THE GAY FAITH

THE GAY FAITH

Christ, Scripture, and Sexuality

M.W. SPHERO

J.D., M.B.A.

HERMS PRESS

NEW YORK ▷ NEW ORLEANS ▷ SYDNEY ▷ OXFORD ▷ TOKYO

First published simultaneously in the U.S. and Europe 2011

by HERMS PRESS

New Orleans, Louisiana & Europe

The right of M.W. Sphero to be identified as the Author of this work has been asserted by him in accordance with the 1976 United States Copyright Act, as well as by the United Kingdom Copyright, Design and Patents Act of 1988.

Cover design by 7grafiks

2 4 6 8 10 9 7 5 3 1

A record for this book is available from the British Library

While every precaution has been taken in the research and preparation of this book, neither the publisher, author, nor any fiduciary parties (named, implied, or otherwise perceived by the reader) assume any personal liability or responsibility, direct or indirect, for errors, advice, opinions expressed or personal points of view, any and all quotations, or omissions; nor for direct or consequential damages or loss resulting from the use, observations, conclusions, or interpretation of any of the information contained herein. This book includes information from many sources and is published for general reference, and is not intended to be a substitute for independent verification when necessary, and neither the author nor publisher is engaged in rendering any psychological, financial, legal, or moral advise. Any mention of an establishment, organization, service, professional person or body, product, association, religion, celebrity, persons living or dead, or figures in the media or the public light neither implies endorsement nor judgment of character by either the publisher or author; and is mentioned for purposes of illustration and the exemplification of points made whose conclusions rest solely on the reader's judgment to make on his or her own initiative.

Send queries to:

queries@hermspress.com

ISBN: 978-09559440-7-9

To all who strive, in one way or another,
with the question of homosexuality
in a world where shades of gray
are perturbed by the egotisms of black and white.

May you find some solace and mental tranquility
within these pages.

Contents

BUT IN ALL THESE THINGS WE OVERWHELM-
INGLY CONQUER THROUGH HIM WHO LOVED
US. FOR I AM CONVINCED THAT NEITHER
DEATH, NOR LIFE, NOR ANGELS, NOR PRINCI-
PALITIES, NOR THINGS PRESENT, NOR THINGS
TO COME, NOR POWERS, NOR HEIGHT, NOR
DEPTH, NOR ANY OTHER CREATED THING,
WILL BE ABLE TO SEPARATE US FROM THE
LOVE OF GOD, WHICH IS IN CHRIST JESUS OUR
LORD.

ROMANS 8:37-39

Preface: Why Read This Book

Too many people have been made to suffer needlessly at the hands of organized religion throughout history simply because they are naturally attracted to and love others of the same sex. In addition to this, there are many sincere people of faith who struggle with the question of homosexuality – on the one hand genuinely desiring to understand and have a sympathetic tolerance towards their homosexual friends or family members, while on the other hand fighting with questions as to what their faith might or might not truly say about the subject.

Conversely, there are still *others* within organized religion who have – whether intentionally or not – forcefully loaded fellow believers (both gay *and* sexually-active, unmarried heterosexuals) with burdens hard to bear – and this without ever lifting a

finger to ease their resultant suffering.[1] Though they
might not intend to do so, by their actions they have
collectively turned millions of people off to the idea
that a healthy and personal faith can be a valued,
rewarding, and active part of their own lives.

As a direct result, many have fallen away from
their intimate faith in God, as they mistake what
often boils down to as misinformation that has been
passed down through religious tradition for truth; to
where they forget about any possibilities of having a
rich and personal faith in God altogether. And yet God
– to those who might believe – has absolutely *nothing*
to do with how religion in general often treats its
innocent bystanders throughout the world on a daily
basis in the first place. For God *is* love, and he who
does not love does not *know* God.[2]

In addition to all of this, there are many within
religious circles who – though very good-hearted and

---

[1] As Jesus Christ himself stated in MATTHEW 23:4-7, on speaking
about religious leaders in his day who behaved in similar
manners:

> They tie up heavy burdens, hard to bear, and lay
> them on the shoulders of others; but they themselves
> are unwilling to lift a finger to move them.

[2] As the apostle John, who wrote the GOSPEL OF JOHN, writes
in I JOHN 4:7-8;

> Dear friends, let us love one another, for love comes
> from God. Everyone who loves has been born of God
> and knows God. Whoever does not love does not
> know God, because God is love.

genuinely sincere in their faith and in their desire to do God's will as they might see it – will mistakingly believe that God either hates or rejects homosexual people – as this is what they have been taught in certain legalistic religious denominations and organizations that have long-forgotten the power of the Gospel and of the cross, by religious leaders improperly trained or completely out of touch with biblical and historic social context as well as with ancient linguistic considerations, by many facets of popular culture that mistake homosexuality for both weakness and a lifestyle choice, by unethical school teachers and insensitive fellow students who do not respect people's differences, by dishonest politicians looking for votes at whatever cost from their own constituency, and by plain old-fashioned bigots – many of whom themselves struggle with doubts about their own sexuality to the point of militantly condemning anything at all to do with homosexuality in today's society as well as in their own lives.

And thus many innocent, good-hearted, sincerely intending, but often misinformed listeners begin to wholeheartedly *believe* the insensitive and uneducated condemnation-fueled few in an unexamined acceptance of lies within a blanket cloud of collective herd mentality.[3] For how can *so many* people be so

---

[3] The concept of "herd mentality" refers to the way in which a mass population so easily accepts as truth whatever is popularly

wrong? But the truth is, they *are* wrong – and this book will tell you why – through the result of years of research and scholarly investigation, decades of experience from professional sources in their respective fields of study, verifiable hard facts, plain black-and-white scripture – as well as from authoritative experts on religion, world history, ancient linguistics, the social studies of by-gone eras and cultures, and other authorities in relevant scopes of study that are additionally referenced to and cited herein.

Although this work is written particularly for the modern-day Christian believer in that it will show the reader just *how and why* the Bible in and of itself (both Old *and* New Testaments) in actuality encourages and validates those who are gay or lesbian to confidently *accept* the fact that they are who they

---

or widely accepted to be such without questioning its validity on a personal level or by individual investigation and free-will. It is the status quo of the majority, the "acceptable norm" of the masses – to where whoever does not prescribe to it may at times be deemed by a dominant societal group to be an outcast, rebel, blasphemer, heretic, infidel, or otherwise "confused" or "misled". An example of this would be Nazi Germany in WWII and the accepted popular *assumption* that the long-suffering Jewish people, the homosexual, and the mentally and physically disabled were inferior simply because the Third Reich had claimed them as such, and because "everyone else" (many of those living in Germany at that time who considered themselves as "Aryan", for instance) seemed to accept such a claim as truth, so that it "must be true" – at least in the eyes of the majority acquiescing to herd mentality. See also Michael Berenbaum, *A Mosaic of Victims: Non-Jews Persecuted and Murdered by the Nazis*. I.B. Tauris, December 1990.

are and move on with their lives – enjoying who
God has made them to be from birth while bearing
fruit for His kingdom – it is also likewise more than
adequate at explaining to others who are coming from
various religious or non-religious backgrounds why
the subject of homosexuality is a reality of life that
is not going to disappear and that can be handled
objectively for the betterment of mankind.

If you *are* therefore from a Christian background,
you may have at some point wondered what Christ
himself may have said regarding homosexuality –
aside from whatever the rest of the Bible might
or might not state.   What does Christ say about
homosexuality, or about gay people *specifically*? The
answer may very well surprise you – despite what
organized religion has erroneously been teaching the
masses for many years.

Consider the Greek word EUNOÛCHOS, for instance
– translated into the English language as *eunuch*.
This word – used both in scripture as well as in
hundreds of non-religious historical and ancient writings – commonly *included* references to homosexual
people[4]. And Christ *himself* defined "eunuchs" not
only as those "made that way by the hands of men",
but *also* as those who were "*born* eunuchs from their

---

[4] See the full explanation of how Christ himself defined the
word *eunuch* in three different ways that included homosexuals
who are *born* gay from their mother's womb in Chapter 5 on
page 77.

mother's womb" – from birth![5] Taking into context
to whom Christ was speaking to at the time,[6] he
knew that his listeners were very much aware of what
categories of people the word "eunuch" referred to –
and implied that those born as such were *meant* to
be born this way by God's purpose and design. He
seems to have plainly been telling the world – once
and for all – that one's sexual preference should be
accepted as a natural part of life,[7] so that if the
significance of accepting oneself as having been *born*
gay was important enough for Christ himself to have
talked about, than should it not be good enough –
accepted, supported, and encouraged – by those of us
in modern times who are bent on encouraging basic
"human rights" and fair play?

But many of those who tend to have a more legalistic and stringent view towards religion will often
skip over Christ's direct defense of gays and lesbians
in MATTHEW 19:12 – as well as other statements and

---

[5] See MATTHEW 19:12.

[6] See also note 34 on page 71 regarding the importance of
considering both context as well as awareness of what an intended
listening audience is familiar with and knowledgeable about in
regards to specific words, phrases, and slang terms – as well as in
regards to cultural norms, practices, and values – used at the time
and place in history when a statement is either spoken or written.
Furthermore, it is vital to look at *who* is making said statement
in like manner.

[7] As Christ stated that those who can accept this should accept
it – on speaking of those who have naturally been born to be
homosexual when defining the term "eunuchs" in MATTHEW 19:12.

examples of his relating to the same which will be explained within this book[8] – either because they simply *will not* consider the possibility that they have been misleadingly preached at and hence unquestioningly following erroneous doctrine from some religious entities over so many years (so that they will not even bother to take but one second to ponder what Christ might have actually meant) – or because they flat-out *refuse* to be receptive enough to consider a different point of view until *they* are the ones who's son or daughter is found hung in a bedroom closet for having had enough of homophobic-driven rejection, judgmentalism, and condemnation from family, friends, schools, work, and religious institutions[9] of so many kinds.

Nevertheless, if you know for yourself – or suspect – that you are either gay or lesbian; if you are heterosexual but are curious to see just what all the fuss is about when religion is mixed in with the topic of homosexuality such as during that awkward dinner conversation you had with your boss a few weeks ago;

---

[8] Such as detailed in Chapter 6 on page 97.

[9] See also the multi-award-winning film which tells the true story of the young Bobby Griffith, who committed suicide after having endured enormous pressure against his sexuality from his religious parents and conservative community – as adapted to television in Katie Ford and Leroy Aarons, *Prayers for Bobby*. Once Upon A Times Films, 2009; and from the book Leroy Aarons, *Prayers for Bobby: A Mother's Coming to Terms with the Suicide of Her Gay Son*. HarperOne, 1996.

or if you are struggling within your Christian faith (or another faith, or no faith at all) because of this topic – or know others close to you who may be struggling with *their* sexuality, and who have as a result become outcasts or are being bullied because of who they are – this book is for you.

If you are not homosexual but are a believer who sincerely wants to know what the Bible – and Christ *himself* – might have to say about this topic in order to become a better follower of God, bear much fruit, and reach the rejected or desperate-hearted friend you might have in mind, than please read on – for "MY PEOPLE ARE DESTROYED FOR LACK OF KNOWLEDGE".[10] For it details just how wrong and misled much of mankind has been throughout world history about the issue of homosexuality – and this with the full support and hearty approval from numerous organized religions, cultures, and kingdoms; where as a result millions have suffered in a myriad of utterly unjust and horrific ways – and are in these modern times *still* being persecuted, socially ostracized, wrongly imprisoned, or murdered at the unmerciful hands of self-exalted bullies, blood-thirsty zealots, self-righteous ostracizers, resentful and sexually-confused yobs, and bigoted cold-blooded murderers[11] – some of whom are

---

[10] HOSEA 4:6

[11] See also M.W. Sphero, *Escaping the Shithole: How and Why to Leave a Bad Neighborhood Once and for All*. Herms Press, 2009.

quick to claim to "know" God, but who in reality prefer to follow the traditions of man instead of the commandments of God – first and foremost of which is to love Him with all one's heart, and one's neighbor as oneself[12] – these who are truly not *of* God... for God *is* love.[13]

For there are many out there who will do such things as these in order to please and win the approval of their own sub-cultures, religious groups, and political comrades at the expense of ignoring the very voice of the Spirit of God; and who will malign basic absolutes of humanity in the name of religion at the expense of the happiness, safety, and well-being of many of their very own children – who never chose to become who they are, but rather by God's grace were

---

[12] As stated in MATTHEW 22:34-40, when the religious leaders asked Christ which was the greatest commandment that one must follow:

> But when the Pharisees heard that Jesus had silenced the Sadducees, they gathered themselves together.   One of them, a lawyer, asked him a question, testing him, "Teacher, which is the greatest commandment in the Law?" And he said to him, "You shall love the Lord your God with all your heart, and with all your soul, and with all your mind – This is the greatest and foremost commandment. The second is like it – You shall love your neighbor as yourself – on these two commandments depend the whole Law and the prophets."

[13] See note 2 on page xii.

given a distinct individuality "from their mother's womb".

If you would like to shatter the egotisms of black and white, and decide for yourself whether a "gay faith" *is* truly possible, than *please* read on. If not for your sake – than for the sake of your loved ones, your children, your neighbor, and your God. For,

MY PEOPLE ARE DESTROYED FOR LACK OF KNOWLEDGE

Chapter One

This is a True Story

The following is a true story about a boy who, at an early age, was by personal choice converted into Christianity. At the tender age of nine, he was already fervently studying the Bible and earnestly seeking God in his own way, without guidance from "the religious". He did not have to do this to be close to God, but his inquisitive mind, and the drive for perfection, led him to this point, and he was content.

From an early age he began to go to church, always looking forward to Sunday services at his local congregation. In fact, he was *so* in love with God and all that He meant to him, that his parents – who *dearly* loved him unconditionally, and out of anxious concern – actually *threatened* to stop taking him to church if he didn't cool it with what they saw as his over-the-top "preaching", reading, and talking about God to everyone who would listen. . . but such was his excitement and fervor for the Love of his life. Of course they did not mean it, but were merely worried about what direction he might be heading in – for it is difficult to understand the passions of youth sometimes... even if they *are* very positive in intent.

As years passed, and he became a bit older, he began to come across many "interesting" – if not somewhat *bitter* – characters. Yes, there were the few genuinely *good* Christians who were wise and who supported him for who he was – in whatever way they might have seen him, I suppose – and than there were those who thought nothing of – dare one say *maliciously* – filling his head with restrictive doctrine and theology instead of the love and power of God. Maliciously... such a strong word. But when you hear some of the stuff *he* heard, and how he was essentially accosted and verbally attacked in the most fake – yet oftentimes *polite* – manners possible, you would know what I'm talking about. Yes, some of you *must* know what I'm talking about.

The boy, now aged thirteen, began to doubt his spiritual fate. For there were now so many rules and regulations presented to him that, as a young teenager, he found it all difficult to accept – especially since he had originally understood the truth and sim-plicity of being close to God without the complications of "organized religion" getting in the way... the faith of a child as was intended from the foundations of Christianity as opposed to being *religious* I suppose –

as Christ himself had put it plainly on many different occasions.[1]

Still, despite the religious stumbling blocks presented to him at this time, he continued to love his God – who he knew loved *him* first – unconditionally and without religious strings attached – and assumed that if older and seemingly "wiser" men told him whatever erroneous things that they told him, and if some of these things were *supposedly* "supported" by the Bible, than they must be true. But through this wearing out of the faithful by those in error, he began to become discouraged and doubtful of God's unending, incomprehensible love for all who seek Him...even for those who don't. And so his faith slowly became not a joy, but a burden that he assumed he needed to carry in order for him to be loved by God. Oh how the wicked of religion become such stumbling blocks to you and I on our path to the kingdom of heaven.

---

[1] As is stated in MATTHEW 18:15-17:

> And they were bringing even their babies to him so that he would touch them, but when the disciples saw it, they began rebuking them. But Jesus called for them, saying, "Permit the children to come to me, and do not hinder them, for the kingdom of God belongs to such as these. Truly I say to you, whoever does not receive the kingdom of God *like a child* will not enter it."

As a result, be started to become more and more fanatical about *organized* religion as opposed to what was always intended by Christ himself – a personal, simple, childlike faith. As a result of putting more trust in organized religion and what those within it had to say, as opposed to keeping his trust and eyes on Christ, he slowly began to become less and less in love with God – mistaking Him for religion rather than who He *really* was... his ever loving, ever patient, ever smiling Heavenly Father who would *never* forsake him... no matter what. But the damage was done. By age fourteen he felt obligated to tell people about his religion in order to "convert" them, and by now he was constantly paralyzed by guilt and fear that he might not be "good enough" for God. By now he was losing his youth, the youth that God Himself had given him to enjoy – in all its mental, emotional, physical, and sexual manifestations. He was even erroneously feeling as though anything negative that happened to him was a sure sign that God was punishing him for not being "good enough".

Yes, the boy now began to quickly lose focus on his trusting and fulfilling relationship with God through the childlike faith that is the *only* way to *know* God,[2] and now focused on organized religion and its by-products – fear and irrational guilt – instead. And

---

[2] See note 1 on the preceding page as well as note 23 on page 45.

so he continued on struggling, while some good people
who's faith was not *religious* but rather spirit-based[3]
began to notice his fanaticism, and thus tried to
help the youth to realize that God wanted him to be
fully human – without being *trapped* within religion
– and this ironically enough by people in his own
church who themselves *truly* loved God in spirit and
in truth. And although these people also read the
Bible and prayed, they themselves were not ruled
by dogmas and religion, but were rather liberated in
their personal faith to *be themselves*, as God would
have them be. But the boy was too young, and too
much of a perfectionist by nature, to let go of legalities,
study, and constant self-condemnation and self-doubt.
And so he continued, maintaining a faith on the one

---

[3] A woman asked Christ, realizing that he was a Jew and
she a Samarian, how she should practice her faith – whether in
accordance to Jewish law and tradition, or otherwise. As is told in
JOHN 4:20-24, the woman said:

> "Our ancestors worshiped on this mountain, but you
> [herein plural in the Greek] say that the place where
> people must worship is in Jerusalem." Jesus said to
> her, "Woman, believe Me, the hour is coming when
> you will worship the Father *neither* on this mountain
> nor in Jerusalem. You worship what you do not
> know; we worship what we know, for salvation is
> from the Jews. But the hour is coming, and is
> now here, when the true worshipers will worship
> the Father in spirit and truth, for the Father seeks
> such as these to worship Him. God is spirit, and
> those who worship Him must worship in spirit and
> in truth."

hand, while burdening himself with religion on the other. What a wretched collision indeed.

It was not until he was sixteen that he finally met the *wrong* people who, although calling themselves "born-again Christians", were nothing more than the self-righteous stumbling blocks of religion that Christ spoke of on many occasions.[4] First came the preacher who told the boy, who was now aware of his sexuality, that homosexuality was evil and against the Bible. Furthermore, he assured the boy, who by now had finally experimented in his youth – as is right, just, and natural – that if he continued on "being gay", that God would surely punish him and give him AIDS.

Now instead of the boy realizing that this preacher was caught in religious legalism instead of on the Spirit of God and *His* guidance, and that Christ himself had *never* condemned anyone for being gay – or for having a sexual life for that matter – the boy, like so many others throughout history, became ashamed of who he was and who God had created him to be. He became marred by guilt and fear, to the point of contemplating suicide on several occasions. For he knew he would not change, and yet he wanted to please God. But organized religion had now taken its first predominant blow at destroying not only his faith, but potentially his life as well. Needless to say, his priorities quickly shifted from being a lover of God

---

[4] See MATTHEW 23.

– and realizing His unconditional love, acceptance, and approval of him – to becoming entrapped at being as "good" as he could possibly be... or rather as *religion*, not God, would have him be. His God was slowly taking the back seat – now becoming replaced by organized religion... and fear.

But he continued to persevere in his faith nonetheless. Then, at the age of seventeen, when he was *finally* beginning to re-balance his life and his faith, yet another blow from organized religion came to him. This time in the form of Jehovah's Witnesses, who told the boy that he (and all who were not part of their so-called "Christian" sect... *including* any other Christians from other churches and denominations) would surely perish for believing in a technicality regarding Christ's divinity and other frivolous matters of faith[5]. So here he was once more, having to struggle with doctrine and theology, instead of putting his faith in the Christ that he had known so well.

---

[5] Even though Christ's divinity, as based on the Gospels and detailed fulfillment of Old Testament prophecy, has always been clear... for the reader that *may* be of a Christian faith. See also Appendix C sub-section C.3 on page 214; which speaks in more detail in regards to the divinity of Christ. Furthermore, see also *Freeminds.org: Watchers of the Watchtower World.* ⟨URL: http://www.freeminds.org/doctrine/jesus.htm⟩, which does an excellent and accurate job at disputing the Jehovah Witness arguments; *Ex- Jehovah Witnesses Community of Survivors.* ⟨URL: http://www.exjws.net⟩; as well as Appendix B on page 187; which speaks about what cults are, and how to stay away from them.

But this was a serious accusation by the so-called "religious" yet again, and he was in fear for his soul. And so he struggled, and a year later – after much doubt, frustration, and sleepless nights– he finally came out the other side virtually unscathed. But he was starting to get tired of all this spiritual bullying not by some Satan, but rather by the *religion* and those who professed to be "Christians".

Then, as he was recovering from the attacks of these many religious stumbling blocks, who proclaim themselves as children of God, while through manipulative games being more children of hell than anything else; yet another, final, blow appeared from out of nowhere. And again, not from some "worldly temptation" – whatever *that*'s supposed to mean – nor from the devil *himself* – but by others who *again* called themselves "born again Christians". This time in the form of the "Christian" denomination called the International Church of Christ.[6]

---

[6] Also known as the ICC, ICOC; or sometimes known by the city or town name followed by the phrase "Church of Christ", "Church of Christ Jesus", or "Christian Church" – founded in Boston, Massachusetts (U.S.A.) in 1979 by its leader Kip McKean, who in turn originally came from the *Crossroads* movement...yet *not* to be confused with the United Church of Christ. But please note that many churches that were originally under the leadership of the Boston branch have now broken away and *might* be more moderate – but one's own common sense, good judgment, and intuition must always prevail. See also Appendix B on page 187, which also speaks of other cults to stay away from, such as the new globalised cult ideology of "Super Apostles" that has damaged many individual lives.

Now many of these slaves of religion – though there were also many *good* and genuine people who simply happened to have become deceived and entrapped in their religious order – went around claiming to be the *only* true followers of Christ, that all other Christian denominations were heretical and on their way to hell fire, and that *their* theology was strictly based on the "doctrine and lifestyle of the early Christians" – as if the early Christians judged and condemned as these hypocrites did by going to people's homes after the death of a loved one to tell them that the departed was surely going to hell, for instance.[7]   *Of course* neither Christ, nor his early followers, *ever* did this – for even *he* constantly went out of his way to emphasized the importance of *comforting* the grieving,[8] *not* condemning or making pious assumptions, nor making light judgment upon

---

[7] Such instances are well documented, and well known. See *Triumphing Over London Cults: Education and Counselling on Cults & ICC*. ⟨URL: http://www.tolc.org/⟩; *Reveal*. ⟨URL: http://www.reveal.org⟩ – a site and organization made up of former members of the "Boston / International Church of Christ" (a.k.a. ICC or ICOC) who tell their stories; and *Recovery from the International Churches of Christ: rightcyberup.org*. ⟨URL: http://www.rightcyberup.org/⟩ – which reveals the fallacies of this cult's systems of belief. See also Appendix B on page 187 which speaks about what cults are, and how to spot them before it's too late.

[8] For instance, in MATTHEW 5:4, Christ states:

> Blessed are those who mourn, for they shall be comforted

and in MATTHEW 25:44-45, he says:

others. That is not the love of Christ – but "by their fruits you *will* know them". Yet the boy never saw the evil fruits of those religious wolves in sheep's clothing – for his eyes were clouded by always giving too much trust to just *anyone* calling him or herself a "Christian" – and so his spiritual turmoil commenced yet again.

And again they stated that not only the boy, but *anyone* not prescribing to their version of "Christianity", was in *grave* error, not a true follower of God, and would thus *surely* burn. And this because they stated that anyone that was not physically immersed in water had never been truly "converted", and was thus not a child of God – thus themselves nullifying Christ's *very own* teachings of turning to God by faith *alone* – without ever needing some *physical* manifestation thereof – in spirit and in truth.

Furthermore... conversion? Conversion into *what*? The only time Christ *ever* used the word "conversion" was to state that the religious go *out of their way* to

---

Then they themselves also will answer, "Lord, when did we see You hungry, or thirsty, or a stranger, or naked, or sick, or in prison, and did not take care of You?" Then He will answer them, "Truly I say to you, to the extent that you did not do it to one of the least of these, you did not do it to me."

As can be seen by Christ's own teachings, Christianity – as a *faith* – was founded on love, and the care for the desperate-hearted in our midst. When we neglect or abuse these same individuals, we reject and abuse God Himself... at least that is what Christ made clear by both word and action throughout his earthly ministry.

convert someone, and when they are won over, they make him or her twice the child of hell as the religious vipers themselves are.[9]   There is no such word in God's vocabulary.   God wants our souls by an act of *free will* and through a *simple* faith in Him – by placing our *trust* in Him as our Heavenly Father – and not by some mysterious or bewildering so-called "religious conversion". The boy had *almost* forgotten the truth that the only thing one can be converted *into* is organized religion – thus quickly forgetting that by his faith *alone* he was *already* a child of God since his childhood when he had first put his trust in and opened his door to the only begotten Son of God as his First Love.[10]   And as a result of the actions by these mindless religious vipers in sheep's clothing – he stumbled yet again, and began to doubt his faith. Thank you, organized religion. You who oftentimes cares more about argument and doctrine, than you do about the soul of the sincere at heart.

And so, being the perfectionist that he was, the child began to stumble with self-doubt, confusion, and

---

[9] Again, as Christ *himself* said,

> Woe to you, scribes and Pharisees, hypocrites, because you travel around on sea and land to make one convert; and when he becomes one, you make him twice as much a son of hell as yourselves. MATTHEW 23:15

[10] See also the song *First Love* by Stryper, *Soldiers Under Command album*. Hollywood Records, 1985.

guilt once more. His biggest enemy became *himself*. And his God, albeit there, began to seem more and more like some legalistic God of organized *religion* rather than who He truly is – the caring Father and unconditional *Lover* of the souls of mankind.

As Satan had tempted Christ in the desert, so *Christianity*, in its form as yet another legalistic kind of organized religion *rather than* as a global phenomenon of faith and the genuine worship of God "in spirit and in truth"[11] alone, was again tempting the boy to fall away from his faith once more – and this is *precisely* why Christ had called the religious of his day a "broods of vipers" that go out of their way to convert a soul...to then make him twice the child of hell as they themselves are.[12] But he again continued. He persevered even in this. And finally he went through the other side again, having realized after months of self-doubt and despair, fear and guilt, that these wolves in sheep's clothing were simply full of shit...and God even then was with him – having again carried him through the hell that is called organized religion.

But now he was tired. And the boy soon became a young man. And so the last straw finally came when he sought to go to seminary school to become a preacher. He was accepted, and before leaving to

---

[11] See note 3 on page 5.
[12] See note 9 on the previous page.

another state within the country, he called the dean of the college to explain that he was also a musician who had started numerous "Christian-styled" heavy metal bands, and asked if they would make an exception to their "dress code policy" and let him in with his now very long hair – which was to him a proud crown of glory and of all things metal. The dean flat-out refused in a rather rude, narrow-minded, and corporate-slavish manner... so much for early-days-styled Christianity in a so-called "Christian" institution of learning I suppose.

And the young man, realizing that even Christ himself would *not* have turned someone away – especially for something so trivial and spiritually a *non-issue*, and especially when this was *supposed* to be a "Christian" college – immediately saw the *religiosity* within the hypocrisy. In order to be able to get admitted to the institution, he cut his glorious hair. But the *very next* day, he rightly changed his mind and decided that, for the rest of his life, he would *never* again become *like them*... these hypocrites that had caused him so much grief throughout his youth, now to put additional frivolous rules and regulations on his life in the name of religion. Furthermore, although a preacher with a good and sincere heart had even told him that Christ himself did not make an issue of one's sexuality – so that why should he himself do this – the advice had now come too late. He was simply fed up, and now deliberately made the choice to turn away from God altogether... having mistaken Him for religion.   Enough was enough.   And the frivolous whinings of a legalistically-pious idiot at a religious college had become the straw that broke the camel's back. Sure, it was *nothing* compared to what he had been through... but it broke the camel's back.

The young man, wanting to *make sure* he would never become like them, went further now and turned to what he saw to be "Satanism". He felt the power of darkness, and got a great thrill from it – though darkness is an ingenious traitor, mercilessly betraying all who enter into its embrace... whatever way they might come to it. A bit like a boss who is all welcoming and smiles for the first few weeks from when you start a new job – to then unexpectedly start bullying and humiliating you in front of your co-workers when you have finally settled in... and you have no clue from whence it has all suddenly come from.

But he knew that at least he would never become *like them* again – and this to the point of ritualistically and enthusiastically denying Christ and His love for him – as he attempted to ensure that God would *never* take him back. Furthermore, he now let go full-on and began an extremely busy and oftentimes *very unsafe* sexual life that would make counting sheep a finite method of addition by comparison – and this to "make up for lost time" in his youth – as back then little did he know that God does not concern Himself so much with sex as He does with one's heart and soul – that he had always been free to enjoy his sexual side with God's approval. But even this realization had come too late.

And although he was somewhat happy, productive, and himself – he was *still* the same perfectionist that began to make him into a slave of temporal concepts and illusory standards created by social expectations of all kinds – as having become manifest in the vast education that he acquired in order to supposedly "be somebody", in the search for an unwavering stability in life that bore nothing but continuous undertones of anxiety within the psyche, and in a constant hunger for the oft-times worthless approvals of mankind and resultant unnecessary appeasements that went with it all. But he continued, and for the next decade was successful in many scholastic and life-enriching endeavors nonetheless – in fact more so than most people are in an entire lifetime. But something was always missing.

And so a decade past, and soon thereafter, the young man now came face to face with a new and most frightening crisis that would forever change him… one way or another. Fearing the prophesy of the religious had come true, and *knowing* full well, and without a shadow of a doubt, that he had been exposed *many* times through various encounters where he later learned about the great risks he had taken (as people will not always be honest about their status even though they insist on being unprotected – only later do many find out the hard way), he went for a blood test.

Now not long before this time he had befriended yet another so-called "Christian" slave of religion, who had promised him that he would always be there for him, and that he would especially not fail to go with him for his results. The hypocrite never showed up – neither on the first nor the next five times for medical confirmation that it was in fact, and purely miraculously, negative. Yet through this the young man found in himself the courage he never knew he had to face such a *monstrosity* of health-based uncertainty head-on. But he was never alone.

Throughout those six months of testing and waiting, testing and waiting, testing and waiting; the young man despaired at the thought that, if positive, it would have paralyzed his entire life and would have (at least initially) blocked his creativity, on which his dreams and multi-faceted professions were based on... if nothing worse. And what was expected certainly looked definitively bleak – for, as stated, the unsafe risks he had taken were with multiple partners who at the time had not told him of their positive status – but of course it would ultimately have been *his* fault for not protecting himself adequately... and he accepted this.

Then finally, when the last – nothing less than *miraculous* – negative confirmation had come through, the self-claiming "Christian" acquaintance of his – the ignoramus who had once told the young man that he had *never* known God, not even in his childhood, because of his sexuality – now seemed (to add insult to injury) to have become *upset* at the good news – and this to the point of storming out – for he had previously stated that HIV and AIDS is God's punishment for a so-called "deprived lifestyle" (wishful thinking, I suppose), and that by the young man's having previously dabbled in the practices of "darkness", that he would find himself on a "slippery slope" of self-destruction one day.

Such are the odd things the hypocrite did instead of *being there* for the young man in his *desperate* time of need – as Christ *himself* would have expected. If he wasn't there for him, he wasn't there for the very Christ he so fanatically claimed to follow. And if he wished evil on the young man through his self-righteousness, than he wished evil on Christ *himself*.[13] That is not a Christian. That is a legalistically-bent follower of *religion* – as opposed to a genuine follower of Christ – who *defames* and mocks the very name of God by his façade of religious piety and of

---

[13] See note 8 on page 9.

a pseudo-form of "morality". But no matter – all water under the bridge now. For only Christ himself can cure *all* wounds imposed upon us by the many facets of organized religion when we come to him and give him the damages we have been wounded by from the arrogantly pious and traditionally-enslaved blind guides in our past.[14]

Ironically, he was *also* gay... go figure. Than again, had some *organized* form of religion virtually destroyed *him* as well, to where his own conflict between Christ's acceptance and unconditional love towards him versus what he might have been bullied by or heard in some broken church contributed to his own self-contradictions – making him unable to accept himself as God had created him to be, and thus bear fruit – such as being there for the young man – as Christ would have wanted it? Could he have his own story to tell? "I desire mercy, not sacrifice".[15] Well, so maybe he does, but what's done is done...

And that is when the young man finally realized just how much he could not tolerate organized re-

---

[14] As Christ said:

> Come to me, all you that are weary and are carrying heavy burdens, and I will give you rest. Take my yoke upon you, and learn from me; for I am gentle and humble in heart, and you will find rest for your souls. For my yoke is *easy,* and my burden is *light.*
> MATTHEW 11:28-30

[15] See note 9 on page 104.

ligion and its "martyr-styled" stumbling blocks and concubines of heartless deception throughout all these years – and the true evils it represents in the form of envy, the secret hatred and wish that many within it have for the destruction of those who are not *like* them – the judgmentalism, the condemnation, the stench of self-righteousness and haughty mocking of all who are not as they, and the hypocrisy at calling themselves followers of God... when their fruits reveal them as the true children of hell that they really are. But caveat! *Not all* who call themselves religious are as these – there are those who in fact *are* true followers; who do not judge but love, do not condemn but rather support and attempt to understand, are not envious but rather joyful at the good fortune of others, do not wish evil upon but rather cast the evils of self-doubt and desperation away from their friends, neighbors, strangers, and even enemies – through encouragement and support without strings attached – these are the true Christians of the world – and by their fruits you *will* know them – as Christ himself clearly explained.[16]

---

[16] As Christ warned in MATTHEW 7:15-20;

> Beware of false prophets, who come to you in sheep's clothing, but inwardly are ravenous wolves. You will recognize them by their fruits... every good tree bears good fruit; but the bad tree bears bad fruit. A good tree cannot produce bad fruit, nor can a bad tree produce good fruit... so then, you will know them by their fruits.

But beware of the ones who Christ said he would one day state: "Get out of my sight... I never knew you". They are the loudmouths who are quick to condemn in our churches, televisions, and political platforms. And they are many! Beware of these wolves in sheep's clothing, lest they entangle your mind with deceptions that defame the very God they claim to worship... to then slowly lead you away from the One who, unlike these wolves of religion, truly loves you and who will *never* turn you away,[17] nor condemn the one who comes to Him. They are worshipers of a book instead of worshipers of God, exchanging the intuitive teachings of the Spirit of Truth for inapplicable scripture... and exchanging mercy,

---

[17] It is interesting to note the simplicity of faith that Christ taught, which is totally *separate* from religiosity – as he stated such things as:

> No one can come to Me unless the Father who sent Me draws him. JOHN 6:44;

and

> All that the Father gives Me will come to Me, and the one who comes to Me I will certainly not cast out. JOHN 6:37;

as well as

> Truly, truly, I say to you, he who hears My word, and believes Him who sent Me, has eternal life, and does not come into judgment, but has passed from death to life. JOHN 5:24.

He did *not* state we needed to follow a religion, but rather that we could come to a faith in God personally and directly – *without* religiosity.

justice, and love – for their own "politically correct" agendas.

And it was through such justifiable skepticism of organized religion that the young man looked back and realized that the hoped-for prophesies of these hypocrites were nothing but *lies* and *scare mongering* methods at seeking to change him to *their way* of thinking and conducting on a multitude of issues, manners, and behaviors. And it was through his much younger years of studying who Christ *really* was and what he *really* said – knowing that he *himself* condemned such people as these, and loved and healed the humble in spirit and the sincere seeker of truth, and that his mercy was limitless – that he now knew that he himself was a physical testament of that very mercy that he had once erroneously mixed in his mind alongside the evil, bleak, and dark blend of *all* that constitutes organized religion. And he realized now that, although he had deliberately left God over a decade earlier, that God had *never* left him. And despite the religious bastards who had burdened his soul for so long, God *Himself* had released him *even from them* – and from the deceptions they so earnestly cram down the throats of the willing.

Through it *all* – through the worship of all that is Satanic and darkness; through the *countless* unsafe sexual encounters and undeniable exposures to a global epidemic; through the confusions wrought by

those arrogant in spirit; and through the revolt of the
heart and soul *far away* from his First Love – Christ
himself – God had *stood by him,* carrying him in His
arms... even then! Never failing. Never forsaking his
side.

Even when the self-labeled "Christians" mocked
and judged – even when they had prematurely not
only secretly wished for, but declared him as condemned, unloved, and a supposed "lover of evil" and
a lost cause – even when they wrongly perceived
his creative profession as diabolical, "scary", or "of
ulterior motives" – God had carried him through
it all... protecting him as his rebellious child, his
prodigal son, his black sheep... who He loved, and
who He would *never* let go. And that is why God
is greater than *all of them* put together. That's why
He is greater than the modern-day "religious" zealot,
greater than any religion this world has ever or *will*
ever see... and greater than any philosophy mankind
will ever observe. And that is why the young man
now follows His Friend... not as his God, but as his
Heavenly Father.

This book is first and foremost dedicated to that
very special young man and his First Love – as well as
to the love in his life that his First Love has lovingly
given him, Panda Bear – in spirit and in truth.

Chapter Two

The Bible is not *Anti-gay...Despite Popular Opinion*

The claim made by the major organized systems of religion that homosexuality is a "chosen *behavioral* lifestyle" is oftentimes an illogical and unsubstantiated strategy to justify their own biases against their many homosexual neighbors (and oftentimes towards their very own children) in the forms of both overt as well as hidden homophobia and ill-intended injustices of many kinds – these outright prejudices often manifesting themselves in schools, workplaces, places of worship, neighborhoods,[1] and whole communities. As a result, many innocent and well-intended people involved in said religions begin to believe that this claim is true, and will take a black and white approach to the subject of homosexuality while inwardly not truly knowing whether it is right

---

[1] See also Sphero (as in n. 11 on page xviii).

or wrong to hold to the opinions that they have
adopted for such a long time.

Nevertheless, such intolerance *cannot* be legitimately justified by what the Bible states – and this
book will show you why in great detail. As such, it
considers the arguments made by those that attempt
to *force* the Judeo-Christian Bible to support their
assumptions, and explains how the sincere analysis
of scripture actually *contradicts* their reasoning and
in reality affirms that some are *meant* to be born as
homosexual by God's intended purpose and plan for
their lives. But the ultimate analysis must consider
genuine love for others, context of scripture, and the
common sense that God has blessed us all with.

Let us first and foremost look into what Christ
himself said on the matter – for those of us who are
of the Christian *faith*... as opposed to the modern-
day so-called "Christian" form of organized religion.
This distinction between a sincere childlike[2] faith
"in spirit and in truth"[3] that focuses on a personal
relationship with God as our spiritual Father and
ultimate life-long Teacher, Protector, and Defender –

---

[2] "And they were bringing even their babies to him so that
he would touch them, but when the disciples saw it, they began
rebuking them. But Jesus called for them, saying, 'Permit the
children to come to me, and do not hinder them, for the kingdom
of God belongs to such as these. Truly I say to you, whoever does
not receive the kingdom of God *like a child* will not enter it.'"
MATTHEW 18:15-17

[3] See note 3 on page 5.

as Christ clearly explained – versus the ritualistic and legalistic aspects of an organized religion – *must* be distinguished, as modern-day Christianity as an *organized* form of religion does not always follow what Christ commanded – foremost being to love God with all one's heart, and one's neighbor as oneself[4] – and oftentimes *completely* contradicts the teachings of Christ himself in a myriad of ways as shamefully observed from the world's viewpoint when focusing its attention onto words and actions of all things "Christian" – which as a result has unfortunately given *genuine* Christianity as a personal, liberating form of *faith* (as opposed to as an *organized* form of religion) an undeserved and erroneous bad name.

As such, specifically in relation to the topic of homosexuality; if *modern-day* Christianity was not being used by many scripturally-careless groups and organizations as a bully-laden *stumbling block*[5] to millions of homosexuals who are yearning to either come to Christ throughout the world, or hungry for fellowship with fellow believers in a safe place where they will genuinely feel accepted and loved – and if gay people were not being deliberately *lied to* and insidiously deceived as to what the Bible truly states and does *not* state about the subject – I believe that countless more gays and lesbians would be pos-

---

[4] See note 12 on page xix.
[5] See note 1 on page 3.

itively ecstatic to make up a significant share of
the Christian faith throughout the world... especially
considering the fact that Christianity – as a *personal
faith* in and of itself (as opposed to as an organized,
legalistic, ritualistic, and *religious* stumbling-block
manifestation of its modern-day self) – is *much more*
supportive, acknowledging, and welcoming of homosexuality than most (if not all) other major belief
systems out there – as will be thoroughly explained
throughout this book as based on what the Judeo-
Christian Bible actually says and does *not* say on this
subject.

Furthermore, as will be shown in the following
chapters, neither the Old *nor* New Testament ever
gets in the way of homosexuality. On the contrary,
both the Old *as well as* the New Testaments of the
Bible actually affirm and acknowledge homosexuality
as being a valid and realistic part of both life and the
real world in general. A part of live that holds no
shame or condemnation whatsoever – but rather love,
dignity, and romance – to those to whom it has been
given.

In addition, the Bible furthermore makes clear
that we are *not* to follow man-made tradition and
re-interpreted dogma, but the Spirit of the Living
God alone – and *His* only begotten living Word. For
it is Christ who *is* the resurrected and living Word

of God[6] – *not* the personal theological commentaries of subsequent followers – and certainly not some of their modern-day television-hero, money-gluttonous, narrow-minded, and obsessively politically-correct contemporaries. It is *he* who has saved – once and for all – those who put their trust on him *through a childlike and sincere faith alone*[7] without exceptions, preconditions, or stipulations – thus nullifying and doing away with such things as religious law and tradition from the Law and the Prophets (the Old Testament law) that had imposed temporary rules on the Hebrew people for a short and specific time in history – such as the outlawing of mixing cotton and wool on a garment of clothing, sowing with two kinds of seed, and plowing with both an ox and donkey together[8] – and which Christ himself said such rules were "made for man"[9] to where we are *no longer* bound by such things as these. Nor are we enslaved

---

[6] See also Appendix C sub-section C.3 on page 214.

[7] See also note 14 on page 18.

[8] See DEUTERONOMY 22:9-11.

[9] As MARK 2:23-27 states:

> One sabbath he was going through the grain fields; and as they made their way his disciples began to pluck heads of grain. The Pharisees [religious leaders] said to him, "Look, why are they doing what is not lawful on the sabbath?" ... Then he [Christ] said to them, "The sabbath was made for humankind, and not humankind for the sabbath; so the Son of Man is Lord even of the sabbath."

– to where we are not bound by man's *religious* traditions. See also note 10 on the following page; as well as note 18 on page 42.

by organized religion itself – with its legalistic and impossible to bear traditions made by man that keep us from focusing on the true commandments of God[10] – namely to love God with all our hearts and our neighbor as ourselves.[11]

As such, through his role as the unblemished sacrificial lamb of God who would take away the sins of *all* who come to him – without exception, whatever one's sexuality – simply by *accepting* his free, no-strings-attached gift of *both* forgiveness *and* an abundant, liberating, and enjoyable life here in this world as well as in the eternal hereafter – we have been *liberated* from such earth-bound religious trivialities, traditions, and man-made legalities.[12] In addition to this, it was Christ *himself* who clearly and explicitly stated that there are some who, by God's

---

[10] As Christ himself clearly said in MARK 7:6-9 & 13;

> Isaiah prophesied rightly about you hypocrites, as it is written,
> 'THIS PEOPLE HONORS ME WITH THEIR LIPS, BUT THEIR HEARTS ARE FAR FROM ME; IN VAIN DO THEY WORSHIP ME, TEACHING HUMAN PRECEPTS AS DOCTRINES.'
> You abandon the commandment of God and hold to human tradition...You have a fine way of rejecting the commandment of God in order to keep your tradition!...thus making void the word of God through your tradition that you have handed on. And you do many things like this. [abridged]

[11] See note 12 on page xix.

[12] See also L. William Countryman, *Dirt, Greed, and Sex: Sexual Ethics in the New Testament and Their Implications for Today*. Fortress Press, 2007.

own will and choosing, are *meant* to be born gay from their mother's womb, and are thus meant to *remain* homosexual and not marry the opposite sex[13] when stating that "there are eunuchs..." – a term which was also used to refer to homosexuals in that day

---

[13] To where Christians who state that homosexuality is "curable" or "treatable", and who in addition try to get homosexual Christians to attend courses to "cure" them of their sexual preference, are inadvertently persecuting Christ *himself* by being stumbling blocks to those who are meant by God to be who they are – sometimes even to the point of ultimately turning them completely off to their personal faith in Christ as a result of such well-intended ignorance. Such actions are akin to what a cult might do [see Appendix B on page 187]. Furthermore, they do the very same thing to straight young Christians by often imposing skewed "contracts" towards celibacy   until marriage [see also Appendix A on page 151], instead of focusing on preaching the Gospel, visiting the sick and prisoner, helping the poor, and being a support to the desperate-hearted. "Whatever you did not do for the least of these, you did not do it for Me." See also note 8 on page 9. As Dr. Countryman has rightly stated:

> Homosexual orientation has been increasingly rec-
> ognized in our time as a given of human sexuality.
> While most people feel some sexual attraction to
> members of both the same and the opposite sex and,
> in the majority of these, attraction to the opposite
> sex dominates, there is a sizable minority for whom
> sexual attraction to persons of the same sex is a
> decisive shaping factor of their sexual lives.   It
> appears that this orientation is normally inalterable
> and that there is no strong internal reason for the
> homosexual person to wish to alter it. To deny an
> entire class of human beings the right peaceably
> and without harming others to pursue the kind
> of sexuality that corresponds to their nature is a
> perversion of the gospel. Countryman (as in n. 12
> on the facing page).

and age[14] – "... who were *born* that way from their mother's womb" in MATTHEW 19:12[15] – this statement to be further examined in greater detail in Chapter 5 on page 77.

And although Jesus Christ states that not the least of the Old Testament scriptures would disappear before all of its prophesies are fulfilled,[16] he was speaking about the fulfillment of Old Testament prophesies regarding both himself as the promised Messiah to all of mankind, and of the future history and fate of the world – and *not* frivolousness of Old Testament law (six-hundred and thirteen in all as found in the Torah and known as the "Holiness Code") that was made by and *for* man.[17]   Again, these

---

[14] MATTHEW 19:12. See note 4 on page 83; as well as a full analysis on Chapter 5.

[15] See also further detailed explanation in Chapter 5 on page 77.

[16] MATTHEW 5:18

[17] This being in reference to frivolous rules such as Kosher dieting, fasting, the mixing of fabrics, same-sex relations (if that is what is correctly meant by the two verses in LEVITICUS in the first place – and this probably in reference to either sexual acts done during the worshiping of idols as was done by the pagans whom the Hebrews lived amongst during that particular time in history [see note 11 on page 39]; or a man having sex with another man who is at the time already married to a woman), sex during a woman's menstruation period, and the like; and not the Ten Commandments – the latter not being mere rules, but rather matters of timeless universal morality. But the former, the six-hundred and thirteen regulations made specifically for the Jews during a certain period of time – when contrasted with matters of morality as ascribed within the Ten Commandments (which mention *nothing* at all to do with either premarital or gay sex

particular laws having once been written *specifically* for the Israelites during a specific time in history over five millennia ago, which are therefore now *not* applicable to either the Jewish people of today, nor to the rest of mankind[18] – these laws being separate and disconnected from the Ten Commandments,[19] which Christ also made a clear distinction from, and which are universal and applicable throughout history to this very day – to which he focused on as the true laws given to us by God (the Ten Commandments, that is) that he again stated can be summed up in a mere two commands – to love God with all one's heart, and one's neighbor as oneself.[20]

Therefore if it is true that you try your best to love your neighbor as yourself by your *actions* (as

but only adultery...this being an affair with one who is *already* married [see Appendix A on page 151]) – are totally different one from another – the former having been temporary measures of survival, the latter being global issues of social order, justice, and love for one's neighbor not by sentiment but in action [again, see Countryman (as in n. 12 on page 28) for a full and clear explanation of these matters].

[18] See also Ibid. – which fully explains this and related matters to do with both sexually-related customs – mostly to do with straight sex by the way – matters of food and diet, fasting, and other rules as being mentioned in the Old Testament that were in fact meant *only* for a certain people at a certain point in time in world history as temporary measures to ensure the continued survival and distinction of the Israelites alone – and which thereafter ceased from being applicable to anyone as the Judeo-Christian Bible clearly explains in the New Testament. See also note 11.

[19] See note 2 on page 36 for the full list.

[20] See note 12 on page xix.

sentiment has nothing to do with it);[21] would you not accept, affirm, support, and *defend* your gay neighbor as you would want – and *need* – to be treated *yourself* in the same manner... especially if you *had* – hypothetically at least – been born gay? Would not homophobia, intolerances, excommunications, exclusions, unjustified condemnations, incitements to violence, work and church discriminations, and ostracisms against gays and lesbians seem very much *against* God's own will from that viewpoint?

Do we not *want* to be loved by others as they love *themselves*? Would we not want to be loved by others as God *Himself* loves us... unconditionally and without strings attached? This *alone* should be sufficient reason for organized religion to begin to not only accept, but to *in* addition actively *defend* and

---

[21] Please also note that, as the book *Love is a Choice* states, "God assumed love of self when He said, 'Love thy neighbor as thyself'" [Robert Hemfelt, Frank Minirth and Paul Meier, *Love is a Choice: Breaking the Cycle of Addictive Relationships*. Monarch Publications, 1990 p.67]. I state this to caution those entrapped by the "religious", in that religion goes against the face of God when it erroneously condemns the love of self. Christ never taught anything of the sort, and any religion that does, I believe, can be compared to the Pharisees, Sadducees, and lawyers of Christ's time who's hypocrisies taught the oppression of self to the complete submission to religious tradition and law – as many major religions do today. On the other hand, Christ is stating that it is not the adherence to religious law and tradition that makes one truly "religious"; but rather sincere faith, and love for others *not* in sentiment, but rather in *action*.

protect its gay and lesbian neighbors as a matter of universal "Christian" policy.

But the command to love one's neighbor as oneself as one of the ultimate commandments from God to all of humanity – without exception – is obviously not sufficient reason for many to repent of their ways in which they have been treating their homosexual neighbors[22] throughout history; so we shall continue to examine what Christ, the Bible, the people written about within it, and God's Holy Spirit[23] – the ultimate

---

[22] Yes, these whom Christ immensely loves and deeply cares for more than the religious can allow their homophobic-tainted selves to realize or admit, lest they would behave quit differently indeed!

[23] Note that Christ reminds us in MATTHEW 23:8-10 to rely on *His* guidance alone, and not on the guidance of man, as he states:

> Do not be called Rabbi [a religious teacher]; for One is your Teacher, and you are all brothers ... do not be called leaders; for One is your Leader, that is Christ.

Furthermore, Christ plainly stated that *his* Holy Spirit – also having called him The Advocate or Helper – would guide us individually into *all* truth, as he said:

> I will ask the Father, and He will give you another Helper [Comforter, Advocate, Intercessor], that He may be with you forever; that is the Spirit of truth, whom the world cannot receive, because it does not see Him or know Him, but you know Him because He abides with you and will be *in* you. I will not leave you as orphans; I *will* come to you...Peace I leave with you; My peace I give to you; not as the world gives do I give to you. Do not let your heart be troubled, nor let it be fearful. John 14:16-18, & 27.

and,

teacher to those who believe and who are *genuinely* willing to listen to His voice without the undertones of religious bullshit – have to say as we continue.

> When the Spirit of truth comes, he will guide you into *all* the truth...He will glorify me, because He will take what is mine and declare it to you. John 16:13-14.

Lastly, in John 10:27-30 Christ states:

> My sheep listen to my voice; I know them, and they follow me. I give them eternal life, and they shall *never* perish; no one can snatch them out of my hand. My Father, who has given them to me, is *greater than all*; no one can snatch them out of my Father's hand. I and the Father are one.

Chapter Three

What the Bible has to Say: The Old Testament

The Old Testament cannot legitimately be used to argue against homosexuality. As will be explained herein, the Torah's Holiness Code[1] does not apply to homosexuality in modern times, and spoke only of keeping the Jewish Hebrews clean from pagan ritualistic practices and customs of societies living amongst them at that time in Jewish history. Aside from this, the Old Testament is silent in regards to homosexuality – although it may actually *defend* homosexuality as seen in the story of David and Jonathan – which will be elaborated on in Chapter 6 sub-section 6.2 on page 105. Furthermore, the account regarding Sodom and Gomorrah cannot be used as an argument against homosexuality because it had absolutely *nothing* to do with homosexuality in the first place – and the Bible itself *clearly* affirms this

---

[1] See note 17 on page 30.

fact as will be seen in detail from page 46 in this chapter.

Let us again consider the Old Testament laws (the Torah's Holiness Code) as distinguished and separate from the Ten Commandments[2] – the latter of which by the way having absolutely nothing whatsoever to say about homosexuality. Said laws – in addition to what has been mentioned in the previous chapter in regards to garments, the mixing of different seeds, and oxen working together with donkeys – *also* included the forbidding of what *some* might argue to have specifically referred to either same-sex intercourse[3] most likely

---

[2] See Exodus 20:1-17 – the Ten Commandments being:

- That we must worship the only true God and Creator of all, who brings the captives out of slavery.

- Not to worship any false gods or idols.

- Not to make wrongful use of God's name, particularly by using His name in an oath.

- Remembering the sabbath day, to keep it holy – and to rest on that day.

- To honor one's father and mother.

- Not to murder.

- Not to commit adultery – which is essentially to have an affair with one who is already married [see also Appendix A on page 151 for a more detailed examination of the same].

- Not to steal.

- Not to bear false witness against one's neighbor; in particularly, not to accuse one's neighbor falsely.

- Not to covet a neighbor's wife or property, possibly to the point of stealing.

[3] See LEVITICUS 18:22 and 20:13.

to do with sexual rites – as having at the time been performed during rituals of idol worship by pagans living amongst the Hebrews[4] – or alternatively to the act of a man having sex with another man who was already married to a woman[5] when taken in context with proper Hebrew language interpretation as well as to time, place, and culture. In addition to this, specific sexual guidelines to do with *heterosexual* sex were also given, some of which does not apply to this day and age as most people would agree[6] – in addition to other rules to do with such things as the mixing of man's and woman's clothing,[7] taking the same woman back after having divorced and re-married,[8] the outlawing of women defending their husbands in violent quarrels by grabbing hold of the enemy's genitals, possessing different weights of measure[9]... and so the list goes on. Yet the breaking

---

[4] See note 14 on page 41.

[5] See note 15 on page 41.

[6] Such as the prohibition against having sex with a woman while she is menstruating (including sharing the bed with her – regardless of whether sex is involved during this time) – as in LEVITICUS 18:19 and 20:18 – and advice not to touch a woman when she discharges from her period for seven days (LEVITICUS 15:19 & 24). See also Appendix A sub-section A.5 on page 173; as well as note 35 on page 73 – both detailing how Christianity as a faith – as opposed to as the organized form of religion that it is today – was always very liberal in regards to sexual differences and varieties of sexual acts in general (both gay *and* straight forms).

[7] DEUTERONOMY 22:5

[8] DEUTERONOMY 24:1-4

[9] DEUTERONOMY 25:11-16

of *any* of these seemingly minor legalistic rules was
described in the Old Testament as being "ritualistically unclean" (and *not* as "abominations" – as has
often been mistranslated);[10] and many of these regulations, as aforementioned, reflected on pagan temple
ritualistic practices involving idol worship as having
been commonly performed by the Hebrew people's

---

[10] Some English Biblical editions translate the word used
(that being *Toevah*) to mean "abomination", which is a total
misinterpretation from the original Hebrew used in both
Leviticus and Deuteronomy. In fact, the correct interpretation
of *Toevah* means "ritualistically unclean". This is because the
"Holiness Code" (the six-hundred and thirteen aforementioned
rules found in the Jewish Torah which include the above Old
Testament books) was written to set the Jewish people apart from
the pagan cultures that surrounded them at a particular time
in history – hence the importance in keeping strict guidelines
as to ritualistic practices. As such, the Hebraic word *Toevah*
does not in fact mean "abomination", but rather "ritualistic
uncleanliness"... such as eating pork for the Hebrew people at
the time – though Christ declared all foods clean [see MARK
7:19]. In contrast, the Hebrew word *zimah*, which is also
translated as "abomination", and which means "intrinsic evil"
or "evil by nature", could have been used in aforementioned
passages in Leviticus, but never was. As such, it is clear that,
even when these passages in the Old Testament mention male-
on-male intercourse, they in fact do *not* call it an "abomination",
but rather an act that is "ritualistically unclean"... despite what
you may have been told. Even so, LEVITICUS 18:22 and 20:13
– the *only* Old Testament passages that could legitimately be
claimed to be speaking of homosexuality directly – seem to refer
not to homosexual acts in and of themselves, but rather to either
homosexual practices during the worship of idols (which was
common at the time in pagan practices), or alternatively to a male
having sex with another male who is already married as some
have suggested. See note 15 on page 41.

pagan and cult-worshiping neighbors[11] – the critical
importance of taking scripture into proper context to

---

[11] LEVITICUS 18:22, and similarly in 20:13. See also note 10
on the preceding page as well as the following quote from
Anita Cadonau-Huseby, *Leviticus: Pagans, Purity, and Property.*
WordPress, 2008:

> The Scriptures recorded Israel's distinctive faith
> and culture, and no where is this more true than
> in the books that dealt with the law, including
> Leviticus...Following the exile...as the people
> moved out into foreign lands among other nations...
> keeping a strong identity mattered for the sake
> of their survival as a nation...While there's no
> condemnation of homosexual acts in the Torah
> outside the Holiness Code; Deuteronomy forbids
> Israel from giving it's children – male and female
> – to serve as cult prostitutes (23:18-19).   In all
> probability there were both male and female cult
> prostitutes which would explain the prohibition of
> homosexual acts in Leviticus 18–20, and therefore
> were a male to lie with a man as with a woman
> the lines of distinction between the practices of
> the Gentile nations and the nation of Israel would
> be blurred.   The issue wasn't about homo-erotic
> behavior in and of itself in this regard but about
> abstaining from anything that could appear to
> mirror Canaanite rituals dedicated to gods other
> than the God of Israel.

Clearly, the early Christians understood these passages in
LEVITICUS to mean what they are: a separation of the early
Jewish people from social norms existing within pagan cultures
surrounding them, and not the casting of judgment or taking a
stance – one way or the other – on the morality of homosexuality
itself. Context, time of writing, and to whom a passage is being
written to is everything – if such things are not considered on
examining scripture, one winds up with 21st century homophobes
within religious institutions who become a stumbling block to God
for millions of people.

time, place, and to whom the text in question refers or is being written to.[12]

These rules that became redundant in their applicability to everyday life millennia ago are mentioned herein because many people in modern times will gladly and without any genuine in-depth examination use the *one* singular rule from the aforementioned "Holiness Code" that at first glance could easily be taken to be in reference to homosexuality – within the long list of the above six-hundred and thirteen others, none of which ever mentioning or inferring anything to do with homosexuality *at all* – which states that "...thou shalt not lie with mankind, as with womankind: it is ritualistically unclean"[13] – to argue against homosexuality...even though all the other rules that have been mentioned were *also* considered to be "ritualistically unclean".

Yet focusing on this particular rule while ignoring the rest (again, such as those regarding garments, cattle, weights of measure, and the like) is to take the statement *completely* out of context to all other

---

[12] See also note 34 on page 71.

[13] As in LEVITICUS 18:22. Some translations have in modern times been brave enough to *erroneously* translate "ritualistically unclean" into "abomination" instead – this error in translation by otherwise competent scholars being an abomination in and of itself.   See note 10 on page 38 for the distinction and explanation as to why the translation of the Hebrew into the word "abomination" is not linguistically accurate as some translators have erroneously done in the past.

surrounding rules that were *all* clearly meant – as a unified set of decrees within the Hebraic Holiness Code – to set the Hebrews *apart* from the idolatry-worshiping practices of those living amongst them[14] – one of which involved *both* homosexual as well as heterosexual sex practices during ritualistic pagan idol worship – these practices having been rampantly widespread amongst the people the Hebrews shared their social environment with at the time these edicts were imposed.[15] To state that the rule that *might* refer to homosexuality is applicable today, while the rest are not, is to pick and choose in a manner that will

---

[14] See Jacob Milgrom, *Leviticus 17-22*. The Anchor Yale Bible Commentaries edition. Yale University Press, 2000. See also note 11 on page 39.

[15] Aside from this, there is even some doubt if the LEVITICUS verses even refer to "homosexuality" *at all* as the primary subject being referred to mainly due to the literal Hebraic (as well as Hebrew to Greek) translations of "as with womankind", which might also be translated as either "wife" or as "woman's [marriage] bed", to where some believe this verse simply states that two men must not sleep together (sexually) if one of them is married to a woman – which would of course be considered adultery [see also Appendix A on page 151]. Thus this reasoning suggests that what the LEVITICUS verses actually do is forbid male–on–male adultery if one of the men is married to a woman. Why else would the term "wife" or "woman" appear here – why not just state that a male should not lie with a male, and stop their? For this reason, many now feel this verse has absolutely nothing to do with homosexuality per se. Nevertheless, whatever the true meaning, this verse was written as part of the six-hundred-and-thirteen other laws making up the Torah's "Holiness Code" for a specific people at a specific time, and did not intend to make any moral judgments about homosexuality in and of itself in one way or another. See also note 18 on the following page.

support one's personal bias against homosexuality – and organized religion has become an expert at doing so to the detriment of its listeners, and to the exclusion of the many who desire to come to Christ just as they are. Why not also keep the rule in the Holiness Code that states that one must not mix both cotton and wool on an article of clothing?

To choose to take *one* rule to be applicable today – one of the over six hundred odd in the Holiness Code that has *as a whole* been made null and void thousands of years ago by God's own choosing,[16] and yet not keep the rest of said decrees, is to commit religious hypocrisy and to choose pious legalism and the traditions of man over the commandments of God.[17] For even Paul *himself* explicitly stated that we are *no longer bound* by the Holiness Code – or "the law" – because he who comes to God and lives in Him lives *by* faith, and faith alone... not by ancient Hebraic religious rule and regulation. In fact, when he says this, he is actually quoting from the *very same* chapter of LEVITICUS in the Old Testament[18] that *also*

---

[16] See note 18.

[17] See also note 10 on page 28.

[18] As stated in GALATIANS 3:10-14, Paul carefully explains – while quoting from *the very same* chapter of LEVITICUS (particularly 18:5) that mentions the passage in question, this the chapter that also states that the Hebrew people would live by the law – that we are *no longer bound* by the law [the Holiness Code], *nor* do we live by it any longer; but that we live by faith, and faith alone – as he explains:

includes the aforementioned rule which at first glance seems to refer to homosexuality... and Paul states that such rules are *not* applicable any longer! So don't let someone try to state that homosexuality is wrong because the Old Testament says so... they are either very misinformed about what the Bible itself actually says, or are being very careless indeed with scripture for their own biased ends – and likely don't care *who* they run over or become a stumbling block to.

But as a friend once explained in regards to her own inhospitable exclusion from religion, when she finally first realized after two decades that of the *many* religious voices she had heard during her teenage years against her being lesbian, that *none* of these voices were ever from God – she states that one day she simply heard Him say – in whatever manner He may talk to us all – "*I* never said those things to

---

For all who rely on the works of the law are under a curse; for it is written, "CURSED IS EVERYONE WHO DOES NOT OBSERVE AND OBEY ALL THE THINGS WRITTEN IN THE BOOK OF THE LAW" [i.e. LEVITICUS]. Now it is evident that no one is justified before God by the law, for "THE ONE WHO IS RIGHTEOUS WILL LIVE BY FAITH." But the law does not rest on faith; on the contrary, "WHOEVER DOES THE WORKS OF THE LAW WILL LIVE BY THEM." Christ redeemed us from the curse of the law by becoming a curse for us – for it is written, "CURSED IS EVERYONE WHO HANGS ON A TREE" – in order that in Christ Jesus the blessing of Abraham might come to the Gentiles [all non-Jewish people], so that we might receive the promise of the Spirit *through faith*.

you – *they* did". Likewise, don't let the *religious*, who are more than happy to use one sentence in the Holiness Code against homosexuals today, while not being willing to therefore follow *all* of the other edicts themselves because they *know* very well that these laws are *not* applicable to anyone in this day and age – make you stumble on your path to God. Their words are *not* God's words...*He* never said those things to you. *They* did. Please think about that for a second if you will.

Furthermore, Christ *himself* described these rules as null and void, unnecessary, legalistic, and having come from the "traditions of man"[19] – or traditions of *organized* religion – and that we are not bound by them any longer – to where we are now free to come to God *personally* and *directly* as He *Himself* draws us[20] without following or adhering to religious, traditional, and legalistic nonsense whatsoever.[21]

Can *organized* religion say the same thing in this day and age of political correctness, hypocritical taboos, pious tradition that leaves the soul empty, religious observance at the cost of the oppression of those who do not follow, the beheading of those who do not submit while blocking the path and persecuting the few who truly love their God – organized religion's

---

[19] See also note 10 on page 28; as well as note 12 on page xix.
[20] See note 17 on page 20.
[21] See also note 5 on page 156

legalities that oftentimes result in self-repression, confusion, mass murders, world-wide terror, the oppression of the sexually-realistic, the envy towards the sexually-active innocent – and the stifling of spiritual liberty, ultimate truth, and a personal faith and trust in our Heavenly Father who has *absolutely nothing* whatsoever to do with such man-appointed and man-made things... as Christ himself stated?   Sorry to seem so over-the-top, but it *is* true, is it not?

Again, the aforementioned six-hundred and thirteen Old Testament Torah-based "Holiness Code" laws are *all* sweepingly done away with through Christ's *separating* mankind from the *religiosity* of religious law by his finished work for all on the cross, to where a relationship with God is now formed by our sincerely turning to Him by faith alone and simply asking Him – as a child would ask a parent for comfort and safety through a child-like faith[22] – to become part of our lives, and believing (putting our trust)[23] on

---

[22] See also note 1 on page 3.

[23] As Christ himself stated:

> While you have the Light, *believe* in the Light, so that you may *become* sons of Light. JOHN 12:36

Please note that the Greek word for *believe* in the New Testament portion of the Judeo-Christian Bible – that being translated from the Greek word *pistis* – means placing one's "faith in", to "trust in", "entrust" or "putting one's trust in", and to "place one's *reliance* upon" – so that a *belief* in Christ simply means to place one's reliance or trust in Christ – which is accomplished by the simple faith of welcoming God into one's life; and *not* through being "religious", nor by tradition or law. It is an act of *will*, as

Him who He has sent[24] – and *not* by such frivolous
works of obedience to *man*'s rules and traditions –
nor through being "religious", pious, and enchained
to the noose of religious rule of *any* kind. These laws
that did not even have anything to do with the Ten
Commandments in the first place – and all to do with
the survival of a nation at a difficult point in time in
world history.

Another of the most cited sections of scripture in
the Judeo-Christian Bible that is *deliberately* misused
by those arguing against homosexuality is the story of
Sodom and Gomorrah in GENESIS chapter 19.[25] But
the truth is, Sodom and Gomorrah had absolutely
nothing whatsoever to do with homosexuality, and
everything to do with the citizens of these two cities'
blood thirst for violence, inhospitality, and an outright
arrogance and resulting neglect for the poor. The
Bible itself says so in various places, both in the Old

---

well as an act of the *heart* – and this with the mere *faith of a
child*. See also note 1 on page 3; and Lockman Foundation, editor,
*Greek Dictionary of the New American Standard Exhaustive
Concordance*. Zondervan, 2000.

[24] As is said in JOHN 6:28-29:

> Therefore they said to Him, "What shall we do,
> so that we may work the works of God?" Jesus
> answered and said to them, "This is the work of God,
> that you believe in Him whom He has sent."

See also note 23 on the previous page for what the word "believe"
is defined as.

[25] See also Philo Thelos, *God is not a Homophobe: An Unbiased
Look at Homosexuality in the Bible*. Trafford Publishing, 2006.

and New Testament – yes, specifically in reference to Sodom and Gomorrah – without mentioning homosexuality in one single reference. Essentially, attempting to provide an argument against homosexuality by using the story of Sodom and Gomorrah has turned out to be one of the most bold-faced and shameful dirty *lies* that the religious have fed the world in modern times.

The account of Sodom and Gomorrah revolves around the story of Lot, who had migrated to Sodom and who was visited by two angels. The people of Sodom, believing Lot's guests to be spies, gathered outside his door and demanded that the angels be brought out of the property, some of whom then stated "... so we can have relations with them." Lot told them he would give them his two virgin daughters instead – something he would not have done if the mob had been entirely composed of gay people, obviously.[26] The crowd was struck with blindness, and Sodom and Gomorrah were eventually destroyed. What those using this story in a pathetic attempt at arguing against homosexuality fail to mention are the following points:

1. All scriptures referring to this story that are strewn throughout the Bible in both the Old *and* New Testaments which specifically list the

---

[26] GENESIS 19:8

actual sins committed by Sodom and Gomorrah
never mention *nor imply* homosexuality in any
manner whatsoever. For example, EZEKIEL 16:49-
50 states:

NOW THIS WAS THE SIN OF YOUR SISTER SODOM: SHE AND HER

DAUGHTERS WERE ARROGANT, OVERFED AND UNCONCERNED;

THEY DID NOT HELP THE POOR AND NEEDY. THEY WERE HAUGHTY[27]

AND DID DETESTABLE THINGS BEFORE ME.[28]

Modern biblical scholars now agree that the
Judeo-Christian Bible makes it very clear that
the *specific* sins committed by these two cities
were arrogance, an appetite for violence, not
being hospitable to foreign guests, the worship
of idols, and being *ambivalent* to the needs of
the poor – as seen here, and as other references
clearly show as we read on – again, *nothing*
whatever to do with homosexuality.

2. ISAIAH 1:10-17 further affirms the above, especially in regards to the worship of idols, the
   violent ways of life and atmosphere in the two
   cities, and their neglect of the less-fortunate, in
   stating:

   HEAR THE WORD OF THE LORD, YOU RULERS OF SODOM; GIVE

   EAR TO THE INSTRUCTION OF OUR GOD, YOU PEOPLE OF GO-

   MORRAH. WHAT ARE YOUR MULTIPLIED SACRIFICES TO ME?

   BRING YOUR WORTHLESS OFFERINGS NO LONGER. INCENSE IS

   AN ABOMINATION TO ME...I HATE YOUR NEW MOON FESTIVALS

   AND YOUR APPOINTED FEASTS...YOUR HANDS ARE COVERED

---

[27] In other words, full of pride and arrogance.

[28] "Detestable things" being in reference to the worship
of idols and false gods – as is what is commonly referred
to as *detestable* acts within the Old Testament almost
exclusively; and as is inferred through the context of the
story of these two cities.

WITH BLOOD. . . LEARN TO DO GOOD; SEEK JUSTICE, RESCUE THE OPPRESSED, DEFEND THE ORPHAN, PLEAD FOR THE WIDOW.[29]

3. Furthermore, the sin of arrogance is *especially* emphasized throughout more than any other in reference to the story of Sodom and Gomorrah, as again seen in ZEPHANIAH 2:9-10:

SURELY MOAB WILL BE LIKE SODOM, AND THE SONS OF AMMON LIKE GOMORRAH. . . THIS THEY WILL HAVE IN RETURN FOR THEIR PRIDE, BECAUSE THEY HAVE TAUNTED AND BECOME ARROGANT AGAINST THE PEOPLE OF THE LORD OF HOSTS.[30]

4. Even Jesus affirms that the sin of Sodom was inhospitality, as he states when he was sending out his disciples to preach the Good News of the arrival of the Kingdom of Heaven on earth; where he says:

BUT WHENEVER YOU ENTER A TOWN AND THEY DO NOT WELCOME YOU, GO OUT INTO ITS STREETS AND SAY, "EVEN THE DUST OF YOUR TOWN THAT CLINGS TO OUR FEET, WE WIPE OFF IN PROTEST AGAINST YOU. YET KNOW THIS: THE KINGDOM OF GOD HAS COME NEAR." I TELL YOU, ON THAT DAY IT WILL BE MORE TOLERABLE FOR SODOM THAN FOR THAT TOWN.[31]

5. Finally, JUDE 7 in the New Testament talks about how Sodom and Gomorrah were destroyed for their people having gone after *"strange flesh"* – biblical and linguistic scholars agreeing this being in reference to the flesh of *angels* that Jude mentions in the previous verse, and clearly not the flesh of man. This because the flesh of man is *not* considered to be "strange flesh" – or *different, other* flesh – as defined in the Greek[32]

---

[29] ISAIAH 1:10-17 [abridged].

[30] ZEPHANIAH 2:9-10

[31] Luke 10:10-12

[32] See Foundation (as in n. 23 on page 46) p. 1532.

in contextual reference to the flesh of another
human. Thus Jude is referring here to humans
seeking to have sex with angels – as seen in
the story of Lot which it directly refers to – and
thus having nothing *whatsoever* to do with any
form of sexual behavior between humans at all –
homosexual or otherwise.

There is therefore absolutely *no* mention – neither
in these verses, nor anywhere else in the Judeo-
Christian Bible either directly or implied – of homosexuality having *ever* been a reason for the destruction
of the two cities of Sodom and Gomorrah in any way,
shape, or form – plain and simple! In affect, Sodom
and Gomorrah's destruction, according to the Bible,
had nothing at all to do with homosexuality – and
everything to do with arrogant pride, a blood thirst for
violence, inhospitality to foreigners, and the neglect of
the genuinely needy.

As such, those who eagerly use the story of Sodom
and Gomorrah to their homophobic ends are simply
changing scripture to suit their *own* biases – and
deceive many in the process.[33] Unfortunately, many
who listen to such unsupported claims take these
bold-faced lies at face value, believing that this is
what the Judeo-Christian Bible truly states without
bothering to look such assertions up for themselves.

[33] See also Daniel A. Helminiak, *What the Bible Really Says
About Homosexuality*. Alamo Square Distribution, 2000.

But I suppose one can't really blame those who believe such falsehoods *too much* – for how may times have *you* heard the bold-faced lie that "Sodom and Gomorrah were destroyed because of homosexuality". If one hears such a thing long enough from pastors, friends, and even the media, one might begin to believe it without feeling the need to even check out such claims for oneself. It is much like going around proclaiming that mankind never walked on the moon – though it happened a mere handful of decades ago – or stating that the Jewish Holocaust never occurred. When people hear such claims long enough from various sources, they begin to actually *believe* such bullshit – pardon my broken French. And few ever bother to seek to correct their mistaken assumptions.

In fact, by simply considering *just how* the fateful story of these two cities has been widely used to brainwash billions into assuming that the Judeo-Christian Bible is against homosexuality should be enough to make it plain to see that the religious have simply lied to the world, and that neither Christ, the Bible, nor any individuals written about within it were ever against homosexuality at all. The common lie being put forth on a global scale that homosexuality is "wrong" or against God is a modern-day deception and divisive stumbling block (much like the erroneous ar-

guments against premarital sex for heterosexuals)[34]
frequently repeated by otherwise honest and well-
intending people, and oftentimes *intentionally* told by
some would-be false prophets with ulterior motives
designed to deceive the world towards their own man-
made dogmas and away from God and the true faith
of Christianity – a faith that was *never* intended to
become an organized form of religion in the first place,
but which has always been – from its inception – a way
of life that is centered on faith, hope, and love... but
the greatest of these is love.[35]   This, the faith that
shall never be marred by pseudo-saints and television
heroes.

In short, Sodom and Gomorrah had nothing to do
with homosexuality, and the Old Testament does *not*
prohibit one from being gay or lesbian... despite what
you might have heard. And now, onto what the New
Testament portion of the Bible has to say about this
topic.

---

[34] See Appendix A on page 151 regarding what the Bible has to
say about premarital sex as clearly distinguished from adultery.

[35] As Paul puts it:

> Love is patient; love is kind; love is not envious or
> boastful or arrogant or rude. It does not insist on its
> own way; it is not irritable or resentful; it does not
> rejoice in wrongdoing, but rejoices in the truth. It
> bears all things, believes all things, hopes all things,
> endures all things. Love never fails... and now faith,
> hope, and love abide, these three; and the greatest of
> these is love. I CORINTHIANS 13:4-8 & 13.

Chapter Four

What the Bible has to Say: The New Testament

The Bible verses from the New Testament – a mere three in total – that are often misused by many in a very weak attempt at arguing against homosexuality, are all written *exclusively* by Paul alone, and *not* by any of Christ's apostles – nor by anyone else that had walked with Christ during his ministry for that matter[1]. If homosexuality had been an issue either for Christ or for the early Christians, surely there would have been clear and decisive statements made to this

---

[1] These verses being ROMANS 1:27, I CORINTHIANS 6:9, and I TIMOTHY 1:10 – all written *solely* by Paul, someone who had never walked with Christ during his earthly ministry – but who turned to Christ decades after his resurrection. It is interesting to note that you never find Peter, John, Mary – or any other early Christian for that matter – speaking against homosexuality in any way... ever. Not to say that Paul did so, as you may also conclude on reading this chapter – but this is nonetheless a noteworthy fact to mention. For if homosexuality had been an issue, would it not have been mentioned by *other* writers of the New Testament – especially by those who actually lived, breathed, and walked with Christ all the way through to his crucifixion and resurrection?

affect... which of course is *not* the case, or else today's modern fundamentalists would be using more than a mere three passages from Paul to attempt to argue against homosexuality in the first place. Apparently they cannot find any more than these in the New Testament, and neither can I... plain and simple.

And although a very small number of modernized, *post*-1900 Bible translations attempt to *erroneously* place the word "homosexual" within two of these three verses for reasons soon to be explained in detail, there were only less than a handful of words that existed at the time of Paul's writings that were available to him that could be translated into today's English word "homosexual" or "homosexuality". Such words included the Greek *arrenomanes* and *erastes*. And yet neither Paul, nor any other New Testament writers, ever used *any* one of these – *ever*.

The same goes for the original Hebrew scriptures of the Old Testament, by the way. No such words were ever used. In short, translations that are faithful to either the original Hebrew or Greek manuscripts of *both* Testaments do not use the words "homosexual" or "homosexuality" – because these words don't actually exist in the Bible.

In affect, Paul never chose to use any terms whatsoever that directly refer to either gay people or to homosexuality anywhere in his writings even though said terms were available for him to use – and this de-

spite what we currently see in a few modern translations today in said two of the three Paulinian verses.[2]
In fact, it is not until 1946 that the word "homosexual"
even *appears* in the Bible at all[3] – this being after

---

[2] Both *arrenomanes* and *erastes* were used by Greek society at
the time of the New Testament writings to refer to homosexuality,
although these words are *never* found in the Bible at all [see also
Dover, *Greek Homosexuality*. Harvard University Press, 1989].
If early Christian writers such as Paul – and *especially* the
writers of the Gospels – genuinely *had* any inclinations against
homosexuality, surely they would have made this crystal clear,
and would have in addition used the *proper* contemporary terms
to name it in their texts... they never did [see also note 34 on
page 71 regarding the importance of heeding attention to both
context and background knowledge]. All the authors of the New
Testament books were master writers and did not beat around
the bush when putting forth their points of view. They were
not stupid men in the least – certainly not as we commonly see
in modernity today. If homosexuality had been an issue in any
manner, they would have been raving idiots not to have stated
this directly and unequivocally. Again, nothing of the sort is
found within *any* original manuscript from any biblical record
whatsoever [see also Appendix C, sub-section C.4 on page 217].
In short, homosexuality is *never* condemned in scripture when
actually looking at the linguistics in the oft and erroneously used
"clobber passages" [see also linguistic analysis – particularly on
the terms *malakoi* and *arsenokoitai* – regarding the same as in
the main text on page 63].

[3] This being the Revised Standard Version (RSV) 1946,
although translators of the same version later decided a more
appropriate translation should be "sexual perverts" – a huge
difference from the word "homosexual" – and therefore changed it
again in the 1971 edition. The New International Version (NIV)
first used the word "homosexuals" in 1973, and a United Kingdom
English translation (the NEB) used the same translation a
few years later. A small number of versions that in the last
decade have attempted to translate the Bible into the most
contemporary sort of English possible (including street slang
interspersed with bracketed additions that are no more than

German psychologists in the late 19th century first began using the word, to where it was eventually translated into the English language by the early 1900's, and to finally be *inappropriately* utilized in said two of three biblical verses – all of which again having been written exclusively by Paul – in a very limited number of modern English Bible translations from 1946 onward.[4]

To put it plainly, Paul *never even used* the word "homosexual" or "homosexuality" – nor any other Greek, Aramaic, or Hebrew word available to him that would somehow even *infer* homosexuality in any direct manner – anywhere in his writings...plain and simple. Anyone who claims otherwise is either

---

editorial commentaries) have recently attempted to do the same – though this being very limited in number to where any reputable translation, such as those that are focused on the literal translations from the Greek into a reader's native tongue, do not include the word...and neither do they include "sodomite" – yet another relatively contemporary word if looking at it from a two millennial standpoint (first used around the early 1600's) that is just as erroneous to use as "homosexual" – especially since Paul actually used the word *arsenokoites*, which had never been previously used, and which began to be utilized by later ancient Greek texts to mean "traders in homosexual slavery"... or "traders of sexual slaves" [see also note 28 on page 68] which again does not refer to homosexuals or homosexuality in and of itself. Assuming that Paul was referring to homosexuality in general is at best an uneducated leap to a wrongful conclusion of what he was talking about if one is sincerely being faithful to linguistic analysis. But more about the use of this term to be examined as we continue in this chapter.

[4] See also John Boswell, *Christianity, Social Tolerance, and Homosexuality*. University of Chicago Press, 1980

not willing to heed deserved attention to linguistic analysis in regards to ancient Greek, or is simply lying to try and convince the world of his or her own personal homophobic agendas.

As stated in this book's Preface, another term that many agree was often used at the time to *include* homosexuals was the word "eunuch",[5] which again was the precise term used by Christ to state that some were *born* "eunuchs" from their mother's womb,[6] and that he who can accept this should indeed accept it[7] – thus indicating that a eunuch who was born as such is *meant* to be, and thus *remain* – by God's own design – a eunuch, and should therefore accept how he or she has been born to be – or alternatively that the world

---

[5] See also note 14 on page 30; note 4 on page 83; and David F. Greenberg, *The Construction of Homosexuality*. University of Chicago Press, 1988. See also a more in-depth analysis of the word "eunuch" as used by Christ in Chapter 5.

[6] As is readily found in any Bible in MATTHEW 19:12. See also Chapter 5 on page 77 in this book for a full examination of this proclamation.

[7] For even Philip explained the Good News of coming to God by faith and without the need for religion to the Ethiopian eunuch without raising questions regarding his sexuality in any way – and wholeheartedly considered him to be a child of God *without* then setting limits, creating needless doubts, or demanding some sort of "change" of lifestyle whatsoever! See ACTS 8:26-39. Note that homosexuals were *also* oftentimes referred to as *eunuchs* [see also note 14 on page 30], and that eunuchs were often chosen to be court officials (as in this case) for such things as being personal assistants to individual members of royalty and their families due primarily to their trustworthiness in not having the desire to pursue the opposite sex. See also note 4 on page 83; as well as Chapter 5 for an in-depth study on eunuchs and homosexuality.

should accept that there are some who are *meant* not
to enter a traditional male-female marriage because
of their sexuality.[8] This will be further explained in
Chapter 5.

But back to Paul's three passages that have only
in modern times begun to be utilized as "clobber passages" against homosexuality. On closer examination
of Paul's statements in question,[9] many experts in
both biblical and ancient history now hold to the
opinion that these in fact have nothing at all to do
with homosexuality *in and of itself* – in that they
refer rather to a form of violent and abusive sexual
force against another human being – whether that
be gay or straight sex – when performed *specifically*

---

[8] See Chapter 5 for a full explanation.

[9] ROMANS 1:27, I CORINTHIANS 6:9, and I TIMOTHY 1:10.
Again, these were *Paul's* opinions – and *not* Christ's, nor
the apostles or other disciples – if he even *meant* to refer
to homosexuality directly which, as previously stated, is *very*
unlikely when looking at the context of these texts – especially
since he mentions – and in ROMANS *describing* in great detail
– ritualistic pagan idol worship.   Furthermore, as the word
"homosexuality" did not exist in the Greek language at the
time of these writings except for the terms *arrenomanes* and
erastes – and Paul uses the word *arsenokoitai* [see also 28 on
page 68] instead of these other terms that would more clearly
have defined homosexuality – it seems clear he was not speaking
about homosexuality as a lifestyle within these verses which
are now commonly (and *erroneously*) used in modern times as
"clobber passages" to wrongly argue against this issue [see also 2
on page 55]. If the New Testament authors had been against
homosexuality in any sense whatsoever, surely they would have
used either of these alternate and more specific words, and would
have used them often... they never did, *not* even once.

during the worship of idols and false gods[10] in the first instance – such as clearly seen in ROMANS 1:18-32[11] where Paul doubtlessly describes what are in essence sexual cult practices where *both* men and women[12]

---

[10] See Luther Martin, *Hellenistic Religions*. Oxford University Press, 1987.

[11] ROMANS 1:26-27 is one of the three "clobber passages" often misused by homophobic preachers to claim that Paul was against homosexuals when he describes ritualistic practices performed during idol worship by what many now believe to have been the Cybelean/Attic Mystery Cult – as well as other similar pagan cults – which was especially popular in Rome during Paul's time, and which had already been around for a few hundred years. When taking these verses into context to what – as well as to *whom* – Paul was writing [see also note 34 on page 71] – namely that he is explaining that, although God's existence is evident in His creation, his intended audience (the church in Rome) were on a daily basis observing many within their community who openly and boastfully refused to acknowledge God as the Creator of all, and instead wholeheartedly worshiped the creation – namely beasts and human/animal-representative idols via violent ritualistic rape – it is clear Paul was speaking of these violent sexual ritualistic practices performed by both men and women members of the Cybelean Cult alongside temple prostitutes which involved permanent bodily mutilations and disfigurements of all kinds... and *not* to homosexuality in and of itself.

[12] Furthermore, it is only after 400 AD where verse 26 is deliberately *misused* to also condemn lesbianism, which again has no grounding whatsoever due to the above arguments. Please note that all arguments within this book apply to both male and female homosexuality as stated before, though this note is given due to how verse 26 has been so abused and misconstrued to attack lesbians in particular when it is clearly speaking of the above cult during Paul's time. See also Tom Hanks, *The Subversive Gospel*. Pilgrim Press, 2000; Matthew Kuefler, *The Manly Eunuch*. University of Chicago Press, 2001; Diana Swancutt, *Disease of Effemination: The Charge of Effeminacy and the Verdict of God (Rom. 1:18-2:16)*. Society of Biblical Literature, 2003.

"exchanged"[13] natural behaviors for unnatural ones to do with *extreme* forms of temple prostitution, violence, and bodily mutilation that would make most of today's "hard-core" porn look like a walk in the park in comparison.[14] It would therefore seem that such references made by Paul really have absolutely *nothing*

---

[13] Like more reputable and true-to-original-language modern translations of today, the *Harper Collins Revised Edition of the New Revised Standard Version* (NRSV) states in its study notes regarding the term "exchanged":

> The repetition of the word *exchanged* is deliberate: moral confusion follows idolatry, as Jewish thought had long maintained.

Harold W. Attridge et al., editors, *The HarperCollins Study Bible, Revised Edition: New Revised Standard Version*. Harper Collins Publishers, 2006.

[14] See note 15 on the facing page below for a full description of what extreme forms of sexual rituals these pagan cult practices involved. Furthermore, biblical scholars write, such as is found in contextual notes in the NRSV, that:

> These verses clearly refer to Gentiles, as seen from the standpoint of Jewish horror of idolatry... some think that Paul here condemns homosexual acts *by* heterosexual people (i.e., unnatural means "unnatural *for them*"); others that he condemns pederasty (sexual activity between adult men and boys). It is questionable whether Paul thought of homosexuality as a condition or a disposition.

Ibid. In other words, as stated in the main text, what Paul is clearly talking about is in context to idol worship – that idol worship invokes all sorts of moral and psychological confusions, and that either heterosexuals should not be having gay sex as it is not natural *for them* (therefore implying that it is natural for those who *are* gay by nature) or that the worship of idols when pederasty is involved is another symptom of the misbehaviors that were prevalent in Greek sub-cultures.

to do with homosexuality from a moral standpoint when taken into context with the topic he was writing *specifically* about in regards to the participants and operations of the Roman Cybelean Cult[15]– and some

---

[15] The Cybelean/Attic Mystery Cult believed in two deities (Attis and Cybele) who *functionally* exchanged sexual roles within Roman mythology – to where the participants would re-enact their sexually-neutral deities' roles in order to *become* more like them – hard-core women worshipers often literally cutting off their breasts to resemble men, and men cutting off *both* their testicles *as well as* their penis in order to be more like women – and allowing willing participants to rape them to the rapist's heart's content – while other temple prostitutes, both young males and females who were often kidnapped and forced into such temple rituals, would be used as sex slaves over and over again without their free-will or consent – though volunteers (namely galli priests and priestesses) were known to willingly give themselves over unreservedly to the religion.

Yes, this was what Paul was speaking of all along in ROMANS 1:18-32, when read in its entire context [see also note 11 on page 59], and *not* the traditional, innocent forms of natural homosexual acts done by consenting individuals – whether in our gay communities, porn sites, or within our homes with the love of our lives – to where the exchange in sexual behavioral norms between men and women related to extreme psychological and physical role reversals during pagan worship rituals, and not to traditional, good-old-fashioned homosexuality. Believe me, *nothing* we see today – not even within the casual browsing of hard-core porn sites in cyberspace – comes even *close* to what Paul was talking about as experienced in cults such as the Cybelean Cult... which moved sex way *beyond* pleasure and into *religious obligation* and *enslavement* – consequently taking the fun away from sex for the participants, where sex turned instead into unpleasant work and duty... that was what he was referring to, nothing more, nothing less. Literary and historical context *is* everything! See also Firmicus Maternus, *The Error of Pagan Religions*. Newman Press, 1970; Will Roscoe, *Priests of the Goddess: Gender Transgression in Ancient Religion*. The University of Chicago, 1996; Hippolytus; Alexander Roberts and

would add possibly to either involuntary prostitution
or the kidnap and keeping of sex slaves via Greek
pederasty[16] when forcibly coerced by the perpetrator
as opposed to where a consensual relationship was
involved – and not to homosexuality in and of itself
when it does not involve the ritualistic worship of
idols, violent rape, or forced-upon sexual slavery.
Furthermore, even modern-day biblical scholars, such
as the editors of the NRSV Study Bible, have stated
in regards to context surrounding ROMANS 1:22-32,
that:

> These verses clearly refer to Gentiles, as
> seen from the standpoint of Jewish horror
> of idolatry....[17]

James Donaldson, editors, *Refutation of All Heresies: Book V.2.*
Scribners, 1903; as well as the excellent scholarly research
by Jeramy Townsley, *Paul, the Goddess Religions and Queers:
Romans 1:23-28.* ⟨URL: http://www.jeramyt.org/papers/
paulcybl.html#_edn4⟩.

[16] This involving the forced rape, kidnapping, and enslavement
of young males that would sometimes take place under Greek
pederasty common at the time in Greek society – though this
was not always forced nor involved unwilling slaves but for
certain violent exceptions that some feel Paul might have been
referring to – and which again, Paul's referring to the same in
these passages would have had nothing whatever to do with any
moral judgment on homosexuality in and of itself. See Dover
(as in n. 2 on page 55); William Armstrong Percy III, *Pederasty
and Pedagogy in Archaic Greece.* University of Illinois Press,
1998; Robin Scroggs, *The New Testament and Homosexuality:
Contextual Background for Contemporary Debate.* Fortress Press,
1983.

[17] Attridge et al. (as in n. 13 on page 60)

Either way, Paul's verses had nothing at all to do with any moral passing of judgment on homosexuality in one way or another – but rather referred to exceptionally forceful and victimizing roles within certain circles at the time involving *both* homosexual and heterosexual pagan ritualistic practices. To state that Paul was giving a blanket condemnation on homosexuality is simply not being true to the original Greek – nor to historical context – and is essentially illogical, non-contextual, and deceptive.

Furthermore, the Greek terms Paul used in I CORINTHIANS 6:9, and again in I TIMOTHY 1:10 – the two other passages by Paul that many again erroneously misuse as clobber passages to argue against homosexuality in modern times – were *malakoi* and *arsenokoitai*. These words have *incorrectly* (one might even say, deceptively, recklessly, or haphazardly) been interpreted to mean "effeminate" – in the case of the term *malakoi* – and "homosexual" or "sodomite" – in the case of *arsenokoit* – in a small number of modern English Bible translations[18] since 1946 within said verses that short-list certain sins that were especially relevant in Greek and Roman societies at the time of Paul's writing – these including the worship of idols, rape, incest, murder, theft, coveting, fraud, and kidnapping.

---

[18] See note 3 on page 55.

Yet let me digress for a moment here before looking further into the true meaning of the two Greek words used by Paul from the above verses and state that – due to such wholly *irresponsible* mistranslations of these two specific verses, Christianity in the likes of a modern-day *organized* form of religion – as opposed to as a sincere personal faith that comes from within and that it was always meant to be *from the beginning* – has in current times *become* one of the greatest stumbling blocks to innocent gay and lesbian people who yearn to turn to Christ in their personal faith – in spirit and in truth. As Christ told "the religious" of *his* time:

> BUT WOE TO YOU, SCRIBES AND PHARISEES, HYP-
> OCRITES! FOR YOU LOCK PEOPLE OUT OF THE
> KINGDOM OF HEAVEN. FOR YOU DO NOT GO IN
> YOURSELVES, AND WHEN OTHERS ARE GOING IN,
> YOU STOP THEM. MATTHEW 23:13

Modern Christianity as an *organized* form of religion is behaving in exactly the same way that the scribes and Pharisees who Christ was speaking to did when he made this statement. For neither the word "ho-mosexuality", nor any word *exclusively* referring to homosexuality alone (this also including "sodomite", which did not exist until the 17th century AD) – was *ever* used in its Aramaic, Hebrew, or Greek equivalent by Christ – *nor* by Paul, nor anyone else for that matter – in the Judeo-Christian Bible[19] – as will continue to be clearly shown in this work. As such, it is simply nothing more than a *diabolical* hijacking of the Gospel by self-seeking homophobic modern-day Pharisees to have translated words[20] having nothing to do with the same to imply any negative moral connotation to gay and lesbian people of today. And as a result of these *intentional*, bias-motivated mistranslations, many uninformed people who cannot be bothered to actually *investigate* what Paul *truly* meant when writing his passages, have become *unintended* stumbling blocks and spiritual maligners of the works of the Holy Spirit on gays and lesbians of today (created by God as who they are). And spiritual – as well as oftentimes *physical* – blood is on the hands of the more knowledgeable and *intending* modern-day evangelicals for their deliberate, cunning, and underhanded deceptions and incitements fueled by hatred and envy[21] – and this not just in their actions against

---

[19] See also note 2 on page 55.

[20] Even prominent biblical scholars, many of whom are not particularly "pro-gay", have nonetheless now publicly *admitted* that the use of the word "homosexual", "sodomite", and similar words are complete mistranslations of these verses. See also Dr. Gordon D. Fee, *The New International Commentary on the New Testament, The First Epistle To The Corinthians*. Eerdmans, 1987; as well as note 34 on page 71; and note 3 on page 55.

[21] See also Rod Brannum-Harris, *The Pharisees Amongst Us: How the anti-gay campaign unmasks the religious perpetrators of the campaign to be modern-day Pharisees*. BookSurge Publishing, 2006.

homosexual people, but also in their crafty and slick manipulations against heterosexuals as well on giving them burdens hard to bear[22] in the form of guilt trips and biblical misinformation regarding such things as premarital sex[23] – and they will have to give an account to God for their boast-filled and unashamed homophobia (*and* heterophobia) when it's all said and done. They, above others, are without excuse. My apologies for such an inhospitable digression.

Anyhow, back to examining what the words *malakoi* and *arsenokoit* refer to in the other two aforementioned Paulinian verses. Let's first take "malakoi", which is *only* found in I CORINTHIANS 6:9 within the small group of *three* New Testament "clobber passages" – the word *sometimes* being completely mistranslated as "effeminate" in *some* English Bibles. This Greek word actually means "soft", such as in reference to "soft clothing" as used consistently in Greek texts, and nothing more. The word is *never* used in original manuscripts of the Greek New Testament[24] – *not anywhere* – to mean homosexuality at all!

Many now agree that what Paul was describing in the list of sins in I CORINTHIANS 6:9 when using

---

[22] See note 1 on page xii.

[23] See also Appendix A on page 151; which thoroughly examines the issue of premarital sex.

[24] See also Appendix C, sub-section C.4 on page 217, which details just how reliable the modern Judeo-Christian Bible is to its original manuscripts – as well as some very interesting and eye-opening facts regarding the same.

the word "soft" – or *malakoi* – was an attitude of "lazy and low morals" – in essence an ambivalent attitude towards true evils done against humanity – and *not* homosexuality in any manner whatsoever – ambivalent morals being one of the undesirable characteristics that he was describing in a person when also including other sins such as theft, coveting, jealousy, fraud, and such within the aforementioned list.[25] I suppose one could therefore say – along these lines of reasoning – that a religious person who either supports or acquiesces to homophobia against gay people – or to heterophobia against our straight youth with deceptive talks against premarital sex[26] and the unneeded brainwash-intending burden of so-called "chastity rings" with the resultant undue pressure to marry, to where they are more likely to marry the *wrong* person due to sexual repression and desperation, especially when they already have enough to worry about in what they face as young Christians in today's ever-growing anti-Christian society without having to additionally deal with such unscriptural nonsense – is him- or herself being very *malakoi* indeed, and would be well advised to repent from these ways before they *themselves* become active stumbling blocks (either in action or through their own inaction)

---

[25] See also Boswell (as in n. 4 on page 56).

[26] See also Appendix A on page 151 which deals with this topic in detail.

towards anyone – regardless of sexuality – who seeks
to come to God and maintain a personal faith in spirit
and in truth within the *real* world in which we live in.
The time is short, and Christianity cannot afford to
continue to be wrongly *perceived* as a sexual downer –
which in reality it is not and was never intended to be
– that turns everyone off who comes across its path.

Furthermore, the word *arsenokoit*, used *only* in
two verses of the entire Bible[27] – and these again *both*
written by Paul in the remaining *two* New Testament
"clobber passages" mentioned above – has been will-
fully and shamefully mistranslated in modern times
to *supposedly* mean "homosexual", which as stated
before is a descriptive noun that many scholars now
agree in reality had to do *not* with homosexuality as a
sexual behavior or of same-sex attraction, but rather
with an injustice done *against* a homosexual – hence
its accurate translation from the Greek to the English language being "trader of homosexual slavery"[28]

---

[27] Again, I CORINTHIANS 6:9, as well as I TIMOTHY 1:10.

[28] Or literally translated to "homosexual slave trader" –
same meaning – hence reflecting on the challenges facing the
early Christians regarding the kidnapping and enslavement
of homosexuals for purposes of pagan ritualistic enjoyment or
private use by those who could afford to buy a sexual slave of their
choosing. Could Paul have *also* been concerned about the personal
safety of homosexual Christians in the early churches, to where
he uses the word *arsenokoit* instead of other words that would
more directly mean "homosexuals"? As stated, it was common in
the Greek and Roman cultures at the time for some to possess
slaves *exclusively* for sexual exploitation, and nothing more – to
where some feel Paul was specifically referring to such practices

...*not* simply "homosexual" nor "homosexuality" in and of itself either as a lifestyle or as who one has been born to be. In addition to this, this very same word – *arsenokoit* – has been recorded as having been used seventy-three times throughout history in ancient non-religious (hence *secular*) Greek texts (only twice by Paul in the aforementioned verses)[29] – *none* of which refer to homosexuality as a way of life in their context, but rather to the aforementioned definitions regarding sexual slavery and rape *alone*.

When interpreting scripture – as in real life – context is everything. Why do so many ignore this fact? Maybe in their zeal to jump to biased conclusions, they simply ignore context altogether – and this at the expense of the suicidal gay teenager down the road who has had enough rejection by his community, or the dead homosexual person beaten by thugs who in turn have the gall to wrongly cite scripture to attempt to justify what they have done. How will it be when they try doing the same in God's presence one day? Good luck to you buddy.

---

of human exploitation – which we unfortunately still see today from time to time. See Martin et al., *Meanings and Consequences. Biblical Ethics and Homosexuality*. Louisville: Westminster Press, 1996; Cantarella, *Bisexuality in the Ancient World*. Yale Press, 1992; Williams, *Roman Homosexuality : Ideologies of Masculinity in Classical Antiquity*. Oxford UP, 1999; Dover (as in n. 2 on page 55); as well as 16.

[29] See full listing in *The Thesaurus Linguae Graecae*. ⟨URL: http://www.tlg.uci.edu/⟩

As such, Paul in fact *never* stated that being gay is wrong in and of itself,[30] and may have actually been actively *defending* homosexual people through these verses by condemning the acts of kidnapping and enslaving homosexuals for purposes of taking advantage of their natural sexuality with the intent at forcing them into sexual slavery – whether for purposes of pagan idol worship within temple prostitution, or for unconsenting and forced-upon pederasty – to where Paul's statements could turn out to have been nothing more than clear-cut condemnations opposing homophobic actions and crimes against homosexuals, especially as these crimes against gay people often took place in order to either supply pagan shrines with enslaved prostitutes to be exploited by both male and female participants, or alternatively to supply wealthier men with private sex slaves when they somehow could not, or would not, enter into consenting homosexual relationships.[31]

Because of this, could it be that Paul was actually one of the first high-profile pro-gay activists of history – whether he himself was gay or not? Heterosexual people *can* be – and oftentimes *are* – activists for gay and lesbian rights, are they not? Anyhow, taking context into account, many now agree that, in these

---

[30] See also note 2 on page 55.

[31] See both note 15 on page 61 in regards to one of these – the Cybelean Cult – as well as note 16 on page 62.

three New Testament passages, Paul is referring to sexual practices by both gay and straight people for purposes of idol worship; Greek pederasty practices when involving the kidnapping, enslavement, and rape of a young male victim;[32] and violent rape and bodily mutilation of both male *and* female shrine prostitutes during pagan temple idol worship by *both* men and women participant-perpetrators.[33]

Whichever way one may see it, Paul never explicitly stated that simply *being* and *living* as a homosexual was wrong in any way, shape, or form – despite how the uninformed stubborn-willed demand the opposite as being the case, and despite how *few* interpreters have erroneously translated *arsenokoit* only in the last century ... even though many of them have now realized their error of interpretation and have corrected this in most modern true-to-original-language translations.[34]

---

[32] See note 16 on page 62.

[33] See note 15 on page 61.

[34] Ernst-August Gutt, a linguistics specialist in Biblical translations, puts it this way on showing the importance of considering context as well as intended reader's knowledge *about* said context by the words being used – and *how* said words are used – with the following example dialogue between a mother and her daughter:

Mother: "What's your new teacher like?"

Daughter: "He rides to school on a motorbike."

If the daughter liked men who rode motorbikes, the mother would know that her daughter liked the teacher. However, if the daughter did not like men who rode motorbikes, the mother would know that the daughter disliked the teacher. Ernst-August Gutt,

Paul never condemns gays or lesbians. The New
Testament does not condemn gays and lesbians. Fur-

*Relevance Theory and Translation: Toward a New Realism in
Bible Translation.* International Meeting of the Society of Biblical
Literature, 2004.

Hence the importance in taking *both* the reader's background
knowledge and context into account. Likewise, one cannot
assume a reference to "homosexuality" in and of itself from texts
that *instead* seem to be speaking of pagan ritualistic practices
involving sex slaves, and where the word "kidnapping" is used
right after *arsenokoit* as we see in I TIMOTHY 1:10, for instance –
where such a context actually *enforces* the idea that what was
being spoken of therein by the use of the word *arsenokoit* –
and by its very own definition – related specifically to "traders
of homosexual sex slaves". It therefore makes perfect sense
from that perspective why Paul would use said word *instead of*
other words that were available to him that more directly meant
"homosexuals". Paul *knew* who he was writing to, and was well
aware that his audience was very familiar with common societal
practices involving such ritualistic pagan rites, enslavements,
kidnappings, and forced-upon sexual slavery. To forcefully
construe "homosexuality" as a blanket definition out of a word
that clearly has never been used to refer to "homosexuality" from
any historical context whatsoever is simply misleading, if not
diabolical. See also note 28 on page 68.

The same can be said of MATTHEW 19:12 in reference to
"eunuchs", where Christ knew to whom he was speaking to,
realizing that his listeners did not have to hear an explanation
of what the *then* common-day definitions of the word included...
to where Biblical readers of modern times must *honestly* consider
whether if in fact Christ was referring to and directly affirming
gay and lesbian people when he stated that "some are *born*
eunuchs from their mother's womb", to where "those who can
accept this should accept it". See Chapter 5; as well as note 4
on page 83; for a fuller explanation of how the word "eunuch"
was defined by Christ as filling three different categories, the
first of which was in direct reference to gays and lesbians having
been born as eunuchs from their mother's womb, to where they
are meant not to marry... though the world must accept this
difference as a God-given reality of life.

thermore, not even the early Christians, nor the apostles of Christ, *ever* condemned gays and lesbians – there is no evidence whatsoever that they *ever* did.[35] So why does much of modern Christianity do so *now*? Why does it do what is *completely* contrary to the calling of Christ and of the early churches? Does it not have *more important things* to do in this day and age – such as feeding the poor, taking care of the sick and dying, healing the broken, preaching the Gospel, and loving the outcast in action? Can it not start to reprioritize its obligations on earth, and *be* the reflection of Christ that it was *meant* to be from the beginning? The time is short. Be faithful to what you have been called for. And leave meaningless man-made dogma behind. Our dogma is the power of the blood of Christ, the love of an amazing Father and Friend, and the meaning of Truth

---

[35] In fact, it was not until the fourth century AD, when the Roman Greco Platonic philosophy began to *casually* push its way into the church, that Christianity as an *organized* form of religion – which was *never* what it was intended to ever become in the first place – began to adopt restricted views on sex in general, which over the centuries developed to where we are today. Neither the early Christians, nor Jesus, nor the Old *or* New Testament...not even Paul *himself*...had such stringent viewpoints towards sex that many Christians now erroneously have due solely to tradition and to what they hear every day in their churches. And this to the detriment of the rest of the world who has been widely misled into believing that Christianity is a "puritanical" religion. It is not, and has *never* been...not true Christianity at least. See Jr. Lawrence Raymond J., *The Poisoning of Eros: Sexual Values in Conflict*. A. Moore Press, 1989.

in a world where deceptions of every kind have taken the place of justice and mercy... not religion and the condemnation of the innocent.

> But if you had known what this means,
> "I DESIRE MERCY, AND NOT A SACRIFICE",
> you would not have condemned the innocent.[36]

Organized religion must stop deceiving the masses into thinking that Judaism and Christianity is anti-gay as based on their scriptures, as this is a lie without any solid foundation to cause confusion, turmoil, repression, and violence towards innocent homosexual men and women – many of whom are in complete love with God their Father, but who have been roughhoused, bullied, and continuously prevented from having a fulfilling relationship with their Creator by the very ones who claim to *know* God... and from being who they were *meant* to be by God's own will and deliberate design. Yet the unconditional love of Christ will never forsake nor condemn these, his very own outcasts and persecuted children of modernity, religion, and strife – whatever the "religious" and the world might say... or do.

> You are the light of the world...
> *be* the light of the world.

---

[36] As stated by Jesus Christ in MATTHEW 12:7.

We reject [homosexuals], treat them as pariahs, and push them outside our church communities, and thereby we negate the consequences of their baptism and ours. We make them doubt that they are the children of God, and this must be nearly the ultimate blasphemy. We blame them for something that is becoming increasingly clear they can do little about.

DESMOND TUTU, ANGLICAN ARCHBISHOP OF SOUTH AFRICA.[37]

---

[37] As quoted in Marilyn B. Alexander, *We Were Baptized Too: Claiming God's Grace for Lesbians and Gays*. John Knox Press, 1996.

Christ Said that Some are Born *Gay*

God intentionally predestined some to be homosexual. As PSALM 139:13-16 states:

> FOR YOU FORMED MY INWARD PARTS; YOU WOVE
> ME IN MY MOTHER'S WOMB. I WILL GIVE THANKS
> TO YOU, FOR I AM FEARFULLY AND WONDERFULLY
> MADE. WONDERFUL ARE YOUR WORKS; AND MY
> SOUL KNOWS IT VERY WELL. MY BONES WERE NOT
> HIDDEN FROM YOU, WHEN I WAS BEING MADE IN
> SECRET, INTRICATELY WOVEN IN THE DEPTHS OF
> THE EARTH. YOUR EYES BEHELD MY UNFORMED
> SUBSTANCE.

To state that homosexuality is a choice is to say that God did not know what He was doing – or that He made a mistake – when he formed the gay or lesbian person in his or her mother's womb. This is akin to stating that heterosexuality, or the desire for the opposite sex, is a choice.

So some will respond to this and state that, though they will *always* have a desire for the opposite sex,

they have a choice as to whether they will act on
that desire – for instance, if they are already married.
But this does not nullify the fact that they *do* have
a desire for the opposite sex, even if they do not
act on it. Therefore they will again respond to this
and state that, though their heterosexuality is not a
choice – they will proudly admit to having been born
as heterosexual – gay people on the other hand *did*
in fact choose to somehow *become* gay, and that this
choice is "unnatural".

But if gay people chose something *so* unnatural
for them, then why would they deprive themselves
of the joys of heterosexual sex? Why would they
then agree to live a life of persecution, insults, and
ostracism in many social and cultural circles, and
suffer at the hands of man. . . for a choice? So they will
turn around and state that, because homosexuals are
so lost, crooked, debauched, or somehow more prone
to "sexual" sin than they themselves are – as self-
righteousness and arrogance begin to be revealed, the
worst of *all* sins – as they continue and finally state
that *all* gay people somehow one day made a conscious
choice to *become* gay – just to be rebellious, different,
to go against the grain, to flip the world off – you
begin to realize that, at the very least, this person
does not know their Bible. . . and probably does not
fully comprehend the vast works and purposes of God
either.

For if that is the case – if in fact everyone was
born as heterosexual *without exception* – than anyone
choosing to *become* homosexual just for the sake of
reasons external to whom they really are, is truly
(and pitifully) denying themselves the *true* sexual
pleasures that they were born with. Life's too short
to deny oneself who one truly is...just for the sake
of it. So we must conclude that either *everyone* –
without exception – is *born* heterosexual, to where
some have become martyrs who simply want to inflict
needless social pain on themselves and be deprived
of any "enjoyable" heterosexual sex life for the rest
of their lives in this one single journey through our
very short time on earth for *essentially* no good reason; or that some *are* in fact gay or lesbian from
birth, to where those on the outside who question
homosexual people's natural-born sexual preference
are simply rather closed-minded, legalistic in their
thinking instead of looking at reality, bigoted against
those different than they might be, or – as is probably
the majority of the cases – genuinely *good* people
who simply believe what they have been hearing from
preachers, teachers, and the media in regards to what
the Bible *supposedly* states about the subject.

God help the closed-minded, legalistic, or bigoted
ones when one of *their* own children turns out to
be gay. Or rather, God help the children *themselves*
– too many of whom have already been sacrificed

to the gods of social intolerance through suicides, murders, and violence-filled lives at the hands of the ignorant religious zombies and hate-mongers amongst us... these who coincidentally usually turn out to be the very *same* people who make even *fellow* heterosexuals suffer through their fervent and radical preaching against *any* form of natural heterosexual sex,[1] who turn out to be the workplace bullies who have themselves deliberately exchanged sexual desire for the worship of wealth and a pseudo-form of power only they seem to be aware of having, and who turn out to be the Hitlers and rapists on our streets who mistake sexual desire for the forced and violent dominion of anyone they can harass and exterminate – having never realized that sex is a natural vehicle from God for self-creativity, the expression of love for your partner, the tint of human friendship and unconditional acceptance towards the beautiful stranger on the street, and the sign of life to those who have all but forgotten that *they still live*. Besides all this, even the animals of our world are *not all* born to be

---

[1] See Appendix A regarding why premarital sex is not against the Judeo-Christian Bible, but is rather a subject used by many of the same bigoted preachers to further repress the masses into their own self-made dogmas – as they make even the heterosexuals amongst them stumble on their relationship to God through their repressive judgmentalisms and brainwashings without apology or remorse.

heterosexual, as many studies have proven.[2] Has not God created all... does God *ever* make mistakes?

Does it not seem more reasonable to conclude that homosexuality *is* in fact something that has naturally been given to some of us... from *birth*? Christ seems to have said just as much – that homosexuality *is* in fact a natural quality given to many from before they were even born. He did not say this was a mistake, but quite the contrary said rather that this

---

[2] For some of us to state that being gay is "unnatural" is to be both unaware of the science of nature, and by that naiveté, to *unintentionally* make ourselves into liars. For it has been proven without a shadow of a doubt in this day and age – as has been studiously observed for centuries – that many animal species, such as the male swan for instance, often develop faithful, long-term homosexual relationships that last for years, if not decades. Furthermore, there have been over one-hundred mammalian species studied where homosexuality is frequently found within their kind, *including* sheep – which is interesting when taken into account the fact that Christ often used sheep as illustrations to tell his parables. Likewise, *at least* ninety-four types of bird species are now known to engage in homosexual sex. In addition, it has been proven that up to fifteen percent of geese pairs are homosexual, and that their relationship is oftentimes monogamous – lasting for up to a decade and a half or more. Such geese have even been shown to display characteristics of grief when their same-sex partner dies. Furthermore, even lions, foxes, deer, zebras, African elephants, bears, squirrels, chipmunks, and vampire bats have been known to engage in homosexual acts. And the bottle-nose dolphin, the killer whale, the harbor seal, the Australian sea lion, and the West Indian manatee have all been shown to be exceedingly active in homosexual activity amongst their kind. See the very revealing book Joan Roughgarden, *Evolution's Rainbow: Diversity, Gender, and Sexuality in Nature and People*. University of California Press, 2009; which deals in great and specific detail with the scientific studies revolving around this intriguing topic.

fact should be *accepted* by those – as he puts it – "to whom it has been given."[3] For Christ *himself* stated that, although they were "made male and female" – so that a man will leave his parents on getting married, when speaking against divorce in MATTHEW 19:3-9 – he is on the other hand crystal clear in the *very next* set of verses when he *then* adds that marriage is *not* meant for everyone, and that there are some who were *meant* to be born *not to marry* – despite how some in fundamentalist circles of major religions will wrongly refute these clear statements with their *own* self-imposed naïve concepts of what a so-called "nuclear family" and "family values" should be defined as – to their own blind-hearted detriment. . . and to the spiritual hindrance of many who hear them.

Furthermore, Christ *twice* repeats that only those who can accept this statement – that it is "better not to marry" – are "those to whom *it has been given*". . . these being the ones who should therefore "accept this" (MATTHEW 19:11-12). If being gay is natural and God-given, than why must we continue to condemn the innocent? More importantly, if Christ has *directly* told mankind that such diversity exists as having been part of God's plan for some of us, than how can we argue with God Himself? Is it because we have been *so* tainted by man's religious traditions (as well as by our own prejudices), that we will gladly go

---

[3] See MATTHEW 19:11.

on about it, and by our own actions *refuse* to accept God-given common sense as well as what the Judeo-Christian Bible *really* says on the matter? May it never be!

Christ stated, in regards to not marrying, that there are some who are in his own words *"born eunuchs"* – the word "eunuch" *not* exclusively referring to castrated men as many people unfamiliar in Greek and Roman history will quickly state, but that in the majority of cases historically refers to those who have *no* sexual desire for the *opposite* sex, but who may be sexually active with the *same* sex... hence the word "eunuch" having been a term that *also* referred to homosexual people in earlier Greek and Roman times.[4] Christ *knew* who he was talking to — being

---

[4] The word "eunuch" referred not only to castrated people, but also to homosexuals, to where Christ included *both* in MATTHEW 19:12. Furthermore, it is a historical *fact* that what people *commonly* referred to as "eunuchs" in those times where whole-bodied individuals with absolutely no "parts" missing whatsoever. Christ's listeners had no doubt about what he was talking about, and understood by his comments that gay people are not meant to marry in the conventional sense of the word, but that they should be *accepted* for who they are – and should likewise accept their homosexuality as it having been given to them by God from birth – as in verse 11 of the same. More detailed studies and analysis of the word "eunuch" as having *included* homosexuals throughout ancient history is given in resources such as Charles Humana, *The Keeper of the Bed: The Story of the Eunuch*. Arlington Books, 1973; Greenberg (as in n. 5 on page 57); Johannes Schneider; Gerhard Kittel et al., editors, *Article on Eunouchos*. Theological Dictionary of the New Testament edition. Wm. B. Eerdmans Publishing Company, 1986; John J. McNeill, *The Church and the Homosexual*. Beacon Press, 1993; and Martti

fully aware that his audience realized *exactly* to whom
the word "eunuch" could refer to – and used it without
hesitation.[5]

Because Christ clearly states that some people
were born this way "from their mother's womb", could
this have been the precise time in which he made
his official stance on homosexuality known to the
world – namely that if God has created you as gay
or lesbian, that you *must* accept who you are and
move on with your life? And if God creates you as
such, could you actually be doing wrong to yourself
by *not accepting* the gift that He has given you –
and this due solely to the often overbearing influence
of skewed and closed-minded ways of thinking by
the insincere and uninformed around you, by sub-
cultural bigotry, and by deceptive traditional taboos
from organized religion? Is it actually *incorrect* in
God's eyes, therefore, that one betray the self that God
has meant for one to be – *despite* what the religious
might say, scream about, protest against, and self-
righteously condemn?

Nissinen, *Homoeroticism in the Biblical World*. Fortress Press,
1998. Furthermore, even ancient secular writers show through
their works that the word "eunuch" *included* homosexual people
in and around the time of Christ. See also Clement Of Alexandria,
Paedagogus III [The Instructor]. Kessinger Publishing, 2004;
Clement of Alexandria, *The Stromata III*. Kessinger Publishing,
2004; as well as note 9 on page 88.

[5] See also the importance of heeding attention to context in
note 34 on page 71.

Furthermore, knowing the homophobic hostility
that might have existed amongst certain circles –
possibly within the Pharisees of organized religion
and such – is this why he adds that "he who is
able to accept this, let him accept it"?[6] Of course
the religious of today will quickly say that it is a
"lifestyle choice". But if that is the case, than why
can't the same be said for heterosexuals? Surely
there are few homosexuals that by choice have *decided*
to live as heterosexuals. . . but that does not change
who they are, does it? Nor does a heterosexual
become gay simply because he may experiment with
homosexuality, does he?

No, a tiger cannot, and *will not*, change his strips.
Why *should* he be miserable being something other
than what he has always been – and will continue to
be – till the day he dies? To try to change him into
a parrot is to become a stumbling block to his own
self-esteem as a tiger, and to desecrate the God who
created him as such. Yet the legalistically religious
does not lift a finger or make a mere *effort* to consider
even this, as he is obsessed at proving himself right at
whatever cost for the sake of ego and pride – even to
the point of *ignoring* the very words of Christ himself
– choosing rather to quote Paul and misinterpret his
mere three passages completely out of context in order
to wrongly condemn homosexuality altogether, which

---

[6] MATTHEW 19:12

is in itself an exercise in self-deception as we have
seen in Chapter 4 – and all this while *deliberately*
failing to *at the very least* take but a moment to
reconsider what Christ *might* have meant in the first
place. No matter, we don't need *them* any longer, when
God Himself is our vindicator.

Christ explicitly stated that some were *meant* to be
gay from birth, as seen here in Matthew 19:12 where
he says:

> FOR THERE ARE EUNUCHS WHO WERE BORN THAT
> WAY FROM THEIR MOTHER'S WOMB; AND THERE
> ARE EUNUCHS WHO WERE MADE EUNUCHS BY MEN;
> AND THERE ARE ALSO EUNUCHS WHO MADE THEM-
> SELVES EUNUCHS FOR THE SAKE OF THE KINGDOM
> OF HEAVEN. HE WHO IS ABLE TO ACCEPT THIS, LET
> HIM ACCEPT IT.[7]

. . . to where he clearly defined and categorizes three
types of "eunuchs":

1. those "born that way from their mother's womb"
   – to where those to whom Christ was speaking
   to would have known that he was referring to
   gay and lesbian people here, as having been
   one of the common definitions of what the word
   "eunuch" referred to in Greek and Roman times
   – again, people having *no* sexual desire for the

---

[7] Matthew 19:12

opposite sex, but who had sexual attractions and physical relations with the *same* sex as previously mentioned; [8]

2. those "made eunuchs by men" – namely castrated men, as is commonly thought of today; and

3. those who, by personal choice and free will, chose to *become* eunuchs "for the sake of the kingdom of Heaven" – in other words, those who have chosen to *remain* unmarried in order to focus on God's work without having to be distracted by responsibilities that come with having and supporting a family.

All of these categories of people to whom the term "eunuch" referred to at the time of Christ, as explicitly enumerated and re-defined by Christ himself – were meant *"not* to marry"; to where, having mentioned the second category (those made eunuchs by the hands of man... in other words, having been castrated), it becomes even clearer that the first category *did* in fact refer directly to those who are attracted to the same sex (i.e. gays and lesbians, as his listeners would have understood it to mean as per the inclusive definition

---

[8] See also note 9 on page 58; note 4 on page 83; as well as Humana (as in n. 4 on page 83); Jeff Miner and John Tyler Connoley, *The Children are Free*. Jesus Metropolitan Community Church, 2002; and Schneider (as in n. 4 on page 83).

of the word at the time), and are thus *not* meant
to marry in the same manner that he previously
described in verse 19:4 in regards to male and female
marriage.[9]

---

[9] As stated in J. McNeill (as in n. 4 on page 83):

> The first category - those eunuchs who have been so
> from birth - is the closest description we have in the
> Bible of what we understand today as a homosexual.

Few modern translations *deliberately* mistranslate the word
eunuch into the word "celibate", though this is an outright lie
from the depths of bigotry to attempt to mislead the reader.
The word that was used in the original – as well as subsequent
copies – of the Greek biblical manuscripts *has* in fact always been
EUNOÛCHOS – as is easily found in reputable Bible translations
of today that are faithful to the original language – which most
are. Anyone who has *any* knowledge whatsoever of ancient Greek,
and of the importance of being faithful to original language, and
who tells you that the word means "celibate", is simply being
misleading... and they are likely doing so *intentionally* in order
to further their own personal biased views against homosexual
people. For even Dr. Robert Gagnon, one of the most vocal
anti-gay Christian authors on the subject, has *himself* publicly
admitted on his website in regards to the word "eunuch" *as* used
by Christ in the above quote of MATTHEW 19:12, that

> Probably "born eunuchs" in the ancient world
> *did* include people homosexually inclined, which
> incidentally puts to the lie the oft-repeated claim
> that the ancient world could not even conceive of
> persons that were congenitally influenced toward
> exclusive same-sex attractions.

Likewise, for some to state that what Christ was referring to
were people who are either "physically incapable" of marriage
due to their having been born sexless, made sexless by others,
or who made themselves sexless – or that it may also mean
those "incapable" of marriage because they are impotent or
handicapped in some way – is again a totally ludicrous claim due
to the fact that neither the original language *ever* suggests this in
any way whatsoever, and because everyone knows that neither

But that is why we have such things as "civil partnerships" or "civil unions" today,[10] to where two people of the same sex will legalize their *partnership* without this romantic covenant having to be called a "marriage" – at least that is the case in some jurisdictions throughout the world. Could it therefore be that, in affect, a legalized joining of two same-sex people should continue to be referred to as a civil union as opposed to as a marriage? Certainly this

---

a physical handicap, nor impotence, *ever* stopped anyone from getting married. Christ *never* said that an impotent or sexually "handicapped" person should not get married. Those who state this, while being aware of ancient Greek, are again telling a bold-faced untruth straight from unfounded assumptions to attempt to deceive many for their own homophobic agendas. We all know that *neither* impotence, nor any physical handicap (even to the point of castration) will *ever* prevent someone from marrying if they wish to do so – and *have* done so – throughout the ages. Such as these are not *only* being anti-gay, but also anti-handicapped in like manner by their prejudicial suggestions... which places them directly *against* the righteousness of God by their own deceptive innuendos. Don't let them lie to you. *Trust* in what Christ has said, and leave those that are nothing more than religious bigots to squander in their own intentionally deceptive filth.

Apologies for such strong wording, but I have *much more* respect even for anti-gay preachers who are *at least* honest enough to admit to the truth as to whom Christ was referring to (such as Dr. Gagnon), than for those who – while calling themselves "Christian" – nonetheless deliberately and with malice aforethought make ludicrous attempts to discredit Christ's words for their own homophobic ends. See also note 4 on page 83 for more on the historic use of the word *eunuch*.

[10] As also existed in a round-about way during the time of Christ, as you will see with the story of Christ's blessing a partnership between a Roman Centurion and his lover who were in fact in a relationship akin to what a civil partnership is today – as explained in Chapter 6 sub-section 6.1 on page 97.

would diffuse much confusion and hostile controversy surrounding this issue from *both* sides in current times, and it would not *in the least* take away from the fact that two people of the same sex who love each other have made a *legally-recognized* and public *commitment* to one another for life if they wish to do so – nor would it diminish either the validity or social rights and status of homosexual couples in the eyes of those who are not homophobic to begin with, and would not add fuel to the homophobic biases of those who will never accept gay people for who they are, no matter *what* one calls such a legal union.

To emphatically *insist upon* using a label called "marriage" could even *unnecessarily* make matters worse for all those involved if we *demand* such a change in order to re-define what many homosexual couples throughout the world *already have* in committed and loving civil partnerships. To state that the term "civil partnership" or "civil union" makes gays and lesbians into second-class citizens is to *admit* that gay rights *still* has a long way to go in certain societies – and thereby to bring into focus the fact that there are other priorities that *still* need to be tackled – such as employment bullying and discrimination of gays and lesbians, homophobic crime and prejudice, and more valid recognitions of legalized unions within various governmental and social departments and services – without the added weight of forcing the

world to change its definition of what a "marriage" means.

Either way, this question should likely not take as much priority as fighting for basic gay and lesbian human rights throughout the world, and actively educating religious circles and the world in general on how the Judeo-Christian Bible has *always been* accepting and supportive of homosexual people. Gay and lesbian people are *already* dying, being violently attacked, maliciously accused and wrongly imprisoned, constantly bullied, and fired from their jobs out there on a *daily basis* as it stands – simply *because of* who they are – and not many people seem to notice or care *whatsoever*! Should not *these* people get priority in our energies on striving to make life better for *them* before tackling what labels we should use for an already legally-recognized union in many nations? Nevertheless, it *is* right and proper that same-sex couples, when entering into a civil partnership, *should* have the same legal rights to social services, immigration status, immediate family hospital visitations, healthcare-related decision-making powers, habitation, and inheritance as their heterosexual counterparts – *regardless* of what label is used to refer to a public and legally-recognized life-long commitment made between two homosexual people.

Likewise, we must *follow* Christ's example and both *acknowledge* as well as *legitimize* gay and lesbian people as *worthy* of our care, attention, unconditional love, friendship, and respect. Encouragingly, there are *many* good Christian heterosexual singles *and* couples within many of our very own churches who do so in this day and age, where by their *actions* they show themselves to be *real* Christians who sincerely follow the teachings of their First Love. "By their fruits you *will* know them."[11] In like manner, as genuine followers of Christ, we must actively *defend* homosexuals throughout the world as Christ *himself* did on other occasions in his ministry – as you will see in detail from Chapter 6.

In the same way that Christ clearly *acknowledged* those who were *born* eunuchs – knowing that his listeners would realize he was speaking of homosexual men and women[12] – and this *without* condemnation as "the religious" do, but rather out of a genuine proclamation of unconditional love – so he *legitimized* their rightful existence and validity in the eyes of their Heavenly Father, and furthermore let us *all* know that the world should *accept* that people *are* different, and that God loves gay and lesbian people enough

[11] Thank you Mom and Dad, Victoria, Japa, Rosey, T.W., and John and Dee – you truly *are* some of the few genuine disciples of Christ in a time where many hearts have otherwise grown cold.

[12] See also Nancy Wilson, *Our Tribe: Queer Folks, God, Jesus, and the Bible*. Alamo Square Distributors, 2000.

to explain that they *also* are His intended children formed from their mother's womb to *be* homosexual from birth[13] – to where they themselves must *also* accept who they have been created to be as well[14] – no matter what the rest of the world, organized religion, or family might say or protest against. After all, why else would he have added that such teachings are given *only* "to whom it has been given"?[15]

Could it be that Christ took the time to mention homosexual people, *acknowledging* their existence as a diverse and *legitimate* part of humanity, and stating that "he who can accept this, let him accept it"[16] because he *knew* that there would come a day in the future where homosexuality would cease from being a non-issue in society (as had for the most part been the case in the Greek and Roman times when Christ spoke these words),[17] and that mankind would attempt to criminalize, ostracize, judge, persecute, and at times even execute those very people who once had been as socially accepted as everyone else?[18]

---

[13] As stated in JEREMIAH 1:5,

Before I formed you in the womb I knew you. . .

[14] See also note 21 on page 32.

[15] See MATTHEW 19:11

[16] See MATTHEW 19:12

[17] See note 33 on page 119.

[18] Christ warned us about how the last days would be before his return to earth specifically so that when we saw certain tell-tale signs occurring, we would not be disheartened nor fail in our faith, but rather *recognize* that he would be coming back for us soon – to

Could he have been speaking more to *us* in modern
times than to his listeners that day – telling us
once and for all what Greek and Roman society had
understood all along – that some *are* born gay and

where he clearly stated that we must hold on, persevere, not panic
nor be fearful, and be happy in life *even when* the rest of mankind
may be in turmoil and confusion [see LUKE 21]. In this regard,
he warned us that some would be killed by the religious, thinking
that they were offering a service to God by doing so [see JOHN
16:2], to where he emphasized that we must not stumble nor be
afraid or terrorized when we see such things occurring throughout
the world [see also LUKE 21:9, 19, & 34; JOHN 16:1; MATTHEW
24:4]. Could such predictions have included what would happen
to *some* innocent gays and lesbians – whatever their religion –
who are often kicked out of some churches in this day and age
[JOHN 16:2]; who are in modern times executed at the hands of
other religions in the Middle East; in addition to those who are
oftentimes brutally attacked and either killed or left for dead due
to violent homophobic hate-crimes prevalent in many Western
countries as well as in many Sub-Saharan nations – many of these
crimes against humanity occurring in the name of religion from
all sides? Could such events be modern-day reflections of just
why Christ was against all organized forms of religion as opposed
to a personal and genuine faith in God in spirit and in truth
alone, as well as all forms of man-made traditional legalisms that
oppress the innocent in countless ways... as he himself said he
was on many occasions? All one has to do is simply read what *he*
specifically talked about and predicted in the Gospels of MATTHEW,
MARK, LUKE, and JOHN; and one will see plainly that this *is* the
case – to where he consistently reminded us that one day he would
come again and bring justice on earth, where such crimes and
terrors would cease to exist and where a new world would be
re-established. He *will* come again in order to prevent mankind
from destroying itself totally – and it seems more and more likely
that he will be coming for *all* who have put their trust in him
– including gays and lesbians of all cultures and backgrounds
throughout the world – very soon indeed. Are *you* ready? See
also ISAIAH 33.

are *still* God's intended children, and that the world should accept this as a fact of life?

Yes, some people *are* born gay by God's intended purpose and design...and He does *not* make mistakes. Christ said so himself, as we have now seen in MATTHEW 19:11-12. Many in modern Christianity – as well as in various other religions – *must* accept this, and move on...lest they continue to be one of the *biggest* stumbling blocks towards innocent spiritual seekers who want to have a personal relationship with God in spirit and in truth. For, as said by Christ himself,

> Whatever you did to the least of these, you did it unto me...whatever you did *not* do to the least of these, you did *not* do unto me.
> MATTHEW 25:40-45

Chapter Six

Both Christ and Scripture Affirm Homosexuality

This chapter will provide further biblical evidence from both Christ's own words *apart from* what has already been mentioned in Chapter 5, as well as from other scriptural accounts throughout the Bible – that show why homosexuality is intended to be a part of life to be accepted by those to whom it has been given. The passages that are looked into herein will provide new perspectives on biblical accounts already familiar to some when re-considering linguistic analysis to original language, historical context, and ancient cultural norms on the same. So let us begin.

6.1 Christ Healed a Gay Relationship

Did you know that Christ healed, and thereby approved of and blessed, a gay couple? Christ healed

a Roman centurion's gay lover – this having been well
recorded in both MATTHEW 8:5-13 and LUKE 7:1-10.

In said accounts of the same event, the centurion
had – through Jewish elders – humbly asked for
Christ to come and heal his servant, and stated that
by Christ's word alone his partner would be made
well from a sickness he was suffering, to which Christ
replied by saying that he had not found such great
faith even among the people of Israel.[1] The term used
in these accounts that directly refers to the centurion's
ill servant is the Greek word *pais*. This term, having
already been more commonly used for centuries before
and up to the time of Christ – both in Greek literature
as well as in daily language – as referring to a "beloved
male lover", "boy" (in a sexual connotation, and referring to either an older teenage or adult lover), or the
younger adult partner in a homosexual relationship[2]
– also alluded to a male servant in other contexts.

---

[1] As stated in the Gospel of Matthew:

> When Jesus heard him, he was amazed and said to
> those who followed him, "Truly I tell you, in no one in
> Israel have I found such faith. I tell you, many will
> come from east and west and will eat with Abraham
> and Isaac and Jacob in the kingdom of heaven, while
> the heirs of the kingdom will be thrown into the
> outer darkness, where there will be weeping and
> gnashing of teeth." And to the centurion Jesus said,
> "Go; let it be done for you according to your faith."
> And the servant was healed in that hour.

Matthew 8:10-13

[2] As stated by Sir Kenneth J. Dover, one of the world's most
prominent scholars in ancient Greek history and literature:

Early Christians reading this account would therefore have had the notion that the Roman centurion came to Christ to humbly ask him to heal his same-sex lover – although this fact is easily overlooked today in modern biblical translations unless one is aware that the word "servant" herein has in fact been translated from the said original Greek term *pais*.

> The Greeks often used the word *paidika* [the diminutive of *pais*] in the sense of "*eromenos*" [see definition below]...The junior partner in homosexual *eros* is called *pais* (or of course, *paidika*). Dover (as in n. 2 on page 55).

The Greek term *eromenos* is in turn described in the following quote:

> In his early twenties the young aristocratic lover (*erastes*) took a teen-aged youth, the *eromenos* or beloved, to bond with and train before going on at about age thirty to matrimony and fatherhood. Armstrong Percy III (as in n. 16 on page 62).

Even one of the most well-known anti-gay apologist, Dr. Robert Gagnon, admits, in relation to the above biblical texts regarding the centurion story, that:

> "boy" (*pais*) could be used of any junior partner in a homosexual relationship, even one who was full grown." Robert Gagnon, *The Bible and Homosexual Practice: Texts and Hermeneutics*. Abingdon Press, 2002.

Furthermore, many ancient Greek writers including Plato, Aeschines, Plutarch, Callimanchus, Thucydides, and Eupolis, commonly used the term *pais* to refer to a same-sex lover in a homosexual relationship. See also Donald Mader, *The Entimos Pais of Matthew 8:5-13 and Luke 7:1-10*. Harland Publishing, Inc., 1998, Homosexuality and Religion and Philosophy; as well as Rick Brentlinger's noteworthy summations of the above on the site Rick Brentlinger, *Gay Christian 101*. Brentlinger, 2011 ⟨URL: gaychristian101.com⟩.

In like manner, in LUKE's account of the same story, it *further* refers to the centurion's male servant in terms of the Greek term *entimos duolos*, which translates as "honored", "distinguished", or "precious servant" – and thus no ordinary *duolos* (or servant) in referring to the person who was ill – which further points to the centurion's sick servant as having been his same-sex partner. This is further confirmed by the fact that the centurion *himself* distinguishes – by the words he himself chose – *other* ordinary slaves of his with the word *duolos*[3] (or ordinary slave/servant) alone, when explaining that they obey his orders and carry out his words – as he explains that Christ's words alone will be obeyed in like manner if only he commands that his servant be healed.[4]

But how can one come to the notion that the centurion and the person he was asking Christ to heal – his "precious servant", or *entimos duolos* – might have been lovers in a same-sex relationship in the first place? At the time, a relationship was often formed through a financial transaction – this being why wives were considered the legal "property" of their husbands, for instance.[5] In like manner, it was common practice for some homosexual Roman centurions, in order to have their same-sex union

---

[3] Matthew 8:9

[4] See also Foundation (as in n. 23 on page 46).

[5] See also Watson E. Mills; Idem, editor, *Mercer Dictionary of the Bible*. Mercer University Press, 1994.

legally recognized, to "purchase" their lover...their so-called *entimos duolos*, or "special servant".[6] It was essentially the common method of choice on which to legally establish what today would be akin to a gay "civil partnership" – to where the partnership was not in fact a slave versus master relationship, but rather a legally-binding and lawfully protected homosexual relationship – this being the only way to officially solidify such a joining of two men in the Roman-ruled part of the world two thousand years ago.

Furthermore, as stated, the centurion initially sent Jewish elders ahead of him to present Christ with this request – to "just *say* the word", and his lover would be healed. What ruling Roman centurion would humble himself to the occupied community and hence make the effort to go to a Jewish rabbi for a mere "servant" or "slave"? Yet for his own precious *entimos duolos* – or same-sex lover – he certainly might.

Although the centurion could have been referring to his servant as his special or "dear slave" because he loved him deeply in a non-sexual manner, it seems much more likely that he was in fact trying to be as sincere with Christ as possible – "coming clean" so to speak – and hence clarifying himself as to the fact that the servant he sought healing for *was* in fact his gay male lover. He was clearly *desperate* for

---

[6] See also Dover (as in n. 2 on page 55); Bernard Sergent, *Homosexuality in Greek Myth*. Beacon Press, 1986.

Christ to heal his servant – for he obviously loved him very much indeed – and did not want to risk appearing as if he was hiding anything if that meant risking rejection... especially since he worked for the occupying Roman Empire, and was humbling himself to ask Christ, an occupied Jew, to have some mercy – and this to the point of sending a delegation of Jewish teachers ahead of him in order for his request to be listened to – though Christ never rejected *anyone* who came to him. For as Jesus has clearly told the world:

> ...ANYONE WHO COMES TO ME I WILL NEVER DRIVE AWAY. JOHN 6:37.

In this regard, when sincerely considering *both* historic and linguistic context as to the well-known common meanings of *pais* as well as *entimos duolos* at the time – the exact terms chosen *both* by Matthew and Luke in the Gospels, undoubtedly knowing very well what sorts of historic and contextual connotations they carried, especially when they could have re-interpreted the conversation to have only used the word *duolos* in place of the above terms as merely pertaining to an ordinary servant and nothing more so as to avoid any potential ambiguity or confusion *if* in fact this had not been a homosexual partnership – and taking into account the centurion's urgency, humility, and openness to use such terms to describe his ill friend; it seems more likely than not that the centurion *was* in fact pleading with Christ to heal his same-sex lover, and not a mere servant that was easily replaceable. Because of this, through the analysis of the very *specific* and significant wording used in these two references to the same story – especially when other alternative and more generalized words were available and were nevertheless *not* used – as well as the circumstantial evidence surrounding both the conversation as well as the parties involved; many now feel that this was in fact a gay relationship, and that Christ made no qualms about it – to where he not only immediately *healed* the centurion's lover, but in addition praised the Roman commander for the great faith he displayed – in comparison to the lack of faith that the "religious" Jewish leaders and peoples around him had seemed to have long lost in the depths of religiosity.[7]

Furthermore, notice Christ's response when the centurion asked him to heal his partner. Christ immediately states, "I will come and cure him" in MATTHEW 8:7. He does *not* say that the centurion needs to change his "lifestyle", or that it is no wonder his partner has become ill, or that they are sinners – like many of those who are stuck within organized religion and legalism today would likely say. No. On the contrary, he states that he will come and heal his

---

[7] See also Miner and Connoley (as in n. 8 on page 87) pp. 46-52.

gay partner right away, and in addition to this praises
the centurion's faith above the supposed "faith" of
those who *claimed* to be religious.

Lastly, Christ tells the crowd gathered around,
who must have at this point been surprised that
he was so welcoming and non-judgmental of a gay
relationship, that "many will come from east and west
and will eat... in the kingdom of heaven"[8] – to where
he pushes the bounds of the kingdom of God to *include*
gays and lesbians. Yes, gays and lesbians who have
put their trust in Christ are *also* part of the legitimate family of God... *despite* what the legalistically
and rigidly stiff-necked religious of today might say.
Christ accepted and affirmed gays and lesbians *by*
example, and we must do the same if we truly consider
ourselves to be *genuine* followers of Christ... lest we
become stumbling blocks who condemn the innocent
and who prevent those who are coming to God to be
at peace in the knowledge that they have in fact *also*
become God's very own children – in spirit and in
truth – through the same child-like faith of a Roman
centurion that manifests itself *apart* from organized
religion.[9]

---

[8] See note 1 on page 98.

[9] As Christ himself put it in MATTHEW 23:13 in regards
to man-made doctrine and religious legalistic traditions that so
easily cause mankind to stumble:

> But woe to you, scribes and Pharisees, hypocrites!
> For you lock people out of the kingdom of heaven.

6.2   A King's Same-Sex Love Affair in the Old Testament

Christ always held David, of his direct lineage,[10] and who would eventually become the king of Israel centuries before Christ's time on earth, in very high regard – never having spoken a negative word concerning him, and even defending him for having gone against the grain of organized religion when he and his friends were on one occasion hungry, to where they decided to take bread out of the Jewish temple to eat, even though it was permissible for only the high priests to do so – calling them innocent in the process, to where he added the statement that has previously been quoted elsewhere:

> BUT IF YOU HAD KNOWN WHAT THIS MEANS – 'I DESIRE MERCY, NOT SACRIFICE' – YOU WOULD NOT HAVE CONDEMNED THE INNOCENT.[11]

Christ spoke these words to the Jewish leaders who were condemning his apostles for having picked heads of grain on the Sabbath, which was not permissible to do so, as according to Jewish law, one must not do any work on the Sabbath. Christ explained to these

---

For you do not go in yourselves, and when others are going in, you stop them.

[10] See MATTHEW 1:1-17.
[11] MATTHEW 12:7

religious leaders that the form of organized religion
(as opposed to a sincere and personal faith in God
the Father) that they were following preferred the
traditions of man rather than God's commandments[12]
– something that could also be stated about today's
Christian-based form of organized religion with its
frequent and often fanatical condemnations against
both homosexuality as well as heterosexual premarital sex,[13] as opposed to the original Christian *faith*
as taught by Christ and the early Christians that
instead concentrated on and preached about God's
love and the love for one's fellow man *without* making
the subject of sex in and of itself an issue whatsoever
in the process.

As Christ showed the leaders of organized religion
at the time what they did not want to accept –
that God's commandments regarding love supersede
any traditions made by man and organized religion
itself – so the story of David and Jonathan is a
biblical fact that modern religious people of today
often do not care to look further into or see it for
what it really is, to where they simply ignore and
do not mention it for fear that it will contradict their
own man-made and unbiblical traditions of condemning homosexuality... all the while forgetting about
truth and the love *for* God and for mankind as being

---

[12] See note 10 on page 28.
[13] See Appendix A on page 151 for further explanation.

more important than their own stiff-necked, religious-borne, and faith-defaming doctrines. What am I on about?

It is strongly believed by many, as explained in the Old Testament, that David and his friend Jonathan came into a romantic and life-long commitment to each other, and that they *were* in fact lovers.[14] Despite this fact, neither Christ, nor any of his followers, ever commented about David's intimate relationship with Jonathan, to where if this had been an issue, surely he would have been clear on providing an opinion about their same-gendered love affair... which of course he never did, because it was obviously never an issue for him to begin with – and this most likely for the same reasons the aforementioned relationship between the Roman centurion and his lover was not an issue for Jesus either.

So let us look closer into what sort of relationship David and Jonathan had – this, a love affair that, though having been well recorded for thousands of years – is for the most part ignored by many in this day and age. The Old Testament book of I SAMUEL 18:1-4 states that

... THE SOUL OF JONATHAN WAS BOUND TO THE

SOUL OF DAVID, AND JONATHAN LOVED HIM AS

---

[14] See Thomas Marland Horner, *Jonathan Loved David: Homosexuality in Biblical Times*. Westminster John Knox Press, 1978; as well as Boswell (as in n. 4 on page 56).

HIMSELF... THEN JONATHAN MADE A COVENANT
WITH DAVID BECAUSE HE LOVED HIM AS HIMSELF.
JONATHAN STRIPPED HIMSELF OF THE ROBE THAT
HE WAS WEARING, AND GAVE IT TO DAVID, AND HIS
ARMOR, AND EVEN HIS SWORD AND HIS BOW AND
HIS BELT.[15]

This covenant between David and Jonathan included
a promise that, if David were to one day become king
in place of Jonathan's father Saul – which eventually happened – that Jonathan would be second in
command to David,[16] and that David would protect
Jonathan's descendants – this agreement having contextually seemed to in addition have overtones of a
romantic commitment entered into between the two,
especially when considering the above choice of words,
the rest of the story, as well as:

JONATHAN MADE DAVID SWEAR AGAIN BY HIS LOVE
FOR HIM; FOR HE LOVED HIM AS HE LOVED HIS
OWN LIFE.[17]

King Saul, who was the first king over Israel as well
as Jonathan's father – *later* proposes the giving of his
daughter away to David in marriage because of his
jealousy towards the attention David is getting from
the populace in regards to military victory over and

---

[15] I SAMUEL 18:1-4.
[16] See I SAMUEL 23:17-18 & 42.
[17] I SAMUEL 20:17

above his own, to where he hopes that – by a union to his daughter, who has *also* fallen in love with David – that she become a "snare for him"[18] – as the narration puts it – in order to destroy David through her. Saul therefore states:

> FOR A SECOND TIME [literally translated as *through two*] YOU MAY BE MY SON-IN-LAW TODAY.[19]

Notice the choice of words that are used. Saul states that David should *again* become a son-in-law to him "through two" – or "for a second time". Had Saul been acknowledging both David and his son Jonathan's pact to each other as what we would today see as a civil partnership?

Later on, because King Saul wishes to kill David as soon as possible for the aforementioned reasons of jealousy – as well as because he fears David might one day somehow overthrow his crown – David and Jonathan make plans to where David will not eat with the king during the new moon festival in order that, when he is missed, Jonathan can assess whether his father truly intends to kill David. As such, they hatch up a plan for David to hide away for three days, and for Jonathan to tell his father the king that David has been called to be with his brethren in Bethlehem

---

[18] As in I SAMUEL 18:20-21
[19] I SAMUEL 18:21

and will be gone for a few days, to where David tells
Jonathan,

> IF YOUR FATHER MISSES ME AT ALL, THEN SAY
> 'DAVID EARNESTLY ASKED LEAVE OF ME TO RUN
> TO BETHLEHEM HIS CITY; FOR THERE IS A YEARLY
> SACRIFICE THERE FOR ALL THE FAMILY'.[20]

Notice again the wording used in the phrase "asked
leave of me", which suggests not only that David
was living with Jonathan, but that they were more
than likely living together as same-sex partners when
again taking into consideration the contextual language used regarding conversations between the two,
the fact that King Saul himself had suggested that
David should be his son-in-law "for a second time"
or "through two" when he proposed that he marry
his daughter,[21] as well as by how the narration itself
takes pains to make clear that these two men had
a deep love for one another – as consistently seen
throughout the entire story which spans both books
of I & II SAMUEL.

But before David is to hide himself in the vicinity
of where Jonathan and his father the king will be
eating, I SAMUEL 20:17 states that,

---

[20] I SAMUEL 20:6
[21] I SAMUEL 18:21

> JONATHAN MADE DAVID SWEAR AGAIN BY HIS LOVE
> FOR HIM; FOR HE LOVED HIM AS HE LOVED HIS
> OWN LIFE.[22]

Furthermore, in regards to the commitment that they had previously made to one another, Jonathan states:

> AS FOR THE MATTER ABOUT WHICH YOU AND I
> HAVE SPOKEN, THE LORD IS WITNESS BETWEEN
> YOU AND ME FOREVER.[23]

Than, on the day of the new moon, Jonathan tells his father that "David earnestly asked leave of me to go to Bethlehem",[24] – as they both had planned to tell King Saul – to where Saul, as his anger for David becomes *openly* manifest, tells his son Jonathan:

> . . . YOU SON OF A PERVERSE, REBELLIOUS WOMAN!
> DO I NOT KNOW THAT YOU HAVE CHOSEN THE
> SON OF JESSE [that is, David] TO YOUR OWN
> SHAME, AND TO THE SHAME OF YOUR MOTHER'S
> NAKEDNESS? FOR AS LONG AS THE SON OF JESSE
> LIVES UPON THE EARTH, NEITHER YOU NOR YOUR
> KINGDOM SHALL BE ESTABLISHED. NOW SEND AND
> BRING HIM TO ME, FOR HE SHALL SURELY DIE.[25]

Does the phrase "to your own shame, and to the shame of your mother's nakedness" suggest that, on top of the

---

[22] I SAMUEL 20:17
[23] I SAMUEL 20:23
[24] I SAMUEL 20:28
[25] I SAMUEL 20:30-31

king's jealousy, and having looked at David as a threat
to his throne, that in addition to this he despised him
for the intimate, if not *romantic*, relationship he knew
full well David was having with his son?

Yes, David and Jonathan certainly *had* a very intimate relationship indeed – so much so that Jonathan
reacts to his father's statement and outright threat
against his friend's life with deep grief – especially
now that he realizes that, for the sake of David's life,
they cannot be seen to be together any longer, and
to where David will have to flee from their common
home within the abode of the king forever. In addition
to this, Jonathan now becomes furious because of his
father's overt disrespect for what appears to have been
the love of his life – as seen here:

> JONATHAN AROSE FROM THE TABLE IN FIERCE
> ANGER, AND DID NOT EAT FOOD ON THE SECOND
> DAY OF THE NEW MOON, FOR HE WAS GRIEVED
> OVER DAVID BECAUSE HIS FATHER HAD DISHON-
> ORED HIM.[26]

Jonathan had established, without a shadow of a
doubt, that his father was planning to kill David. As
such, following the plans he had made with David, he
let David know this straight away. David had to *leave*
the king's dwelling in swift haste... and Jonathan,
whom he *dearly* loved.

---

[26] I SAMUEL 20:34

Jonathan of course followed up on his and his lover's plans, and with a heavy heart too weighty for any mortal to have to bear, let David, the love of his life, know that the king – his *very own* father – was after his life. What a sad, tragic story indeed! As they were saying their final good-byes, I SAMUEL 20:41-42 states:

> AND THEY KISSED EACH OTHER, AND WEPT WITH EACH OTHER; BUT DAVID WEPT THE MORE. THEN JONATHAN SAID TO DAVID, "GO IN PEACE, SINCE BOTH OF US HAVE SWORN IN THE NAME OF THE LORD, SAYING, 'THE LORD SHALL BE BETWEEN ME AND YOU, AND BETWEEN MY DESCENDANTS AND YOUR DESCENDANTS, FOREVER.'" HE GOT UP AND LEFT; AND JONATHAN WENT INTO THE CITY.[27]

As if this isn't enough for two people who adore each other, and who are clearly committed to one another for life to bear – one final blow tragically ended all hopes that they would *ever* see each other again. II SAMUEL 1:26 tells us of David's grief-stricken, and utterly candid reaction, once he learns that Jonathan, the true love of his life, is unexpectedly killed in battle. David, the one who would become Israel's second king, a direct descendant of Jesus Christ *himself*, is *utterly* grief-stricken, and in no uncertain terms proclaims for the rest of history to hear:

---

[27] I SAMUEL 20:41-42

> I AM DISTRESSED FOR YOU, MY BROTHER JONATHAN,
> GREATLY BELOVED WERE YOU TO ME; YOUR LOVE
> TO ME WAS WONDERFUL, PASSING THE LOVE OF
> WOMEN.[28]

Yes... "your love to me was *wonderful, passing* the love of women". The NASB version translates the original Hebrew in this way:

> YOUR LOVE TO ME WAS MORE WONDERFUL THAN
> THE LOVE OF WOMEN.

Such tragic, and very revealing and candid words, as having been recorded – in black and white – in II SAMUEL 1:26. But oh if it had never been so. Not in *this* heartbreaking manner at least.

But does it take the death of a future king's lover – a record that reveals the true nature of an affair from a grief-stricken David that was destined as an eternal witness to his majesty's true thoughts – for us living *thousands* of years later in this Brave New World and very much homophobic 21st century to *see for ourselves* that the love between two men or two women is no less relevant than the love between a loving and life-long-committed heterosexual couple? Does it take the straightforward and direct choice of words of David in his insurmountable grief for us to realize – as is the case with the one who was again at the time to become the future king of Israel, the hand

---

[28] II SAMUEL 1:26

of God having been upon him *even while* he was living such a tragic love story with Jonathan to where it was deemed of him as "acting wisely"[29] – that the Judeo-Christian Bible does *indeed* both value and validate homosexual relationships? Does it even make *any bit* of a difference to us now? But why should it end this way? And why do we continue to let it end this way for so many others who live amongst us and need our love, understanding, and support? And some *still* have the gall to claim that they weren't lovers...just *good* friends. Ha! The *brave* new 21st Century. What a nasty joke...

Anyway, back to cold analytical analysis...I take my hat off to you, friends. Of utmost importance – aside from the obvious "intimacy" – if I may be so "objective" for a moment – that existed between David and Jonathan – is the fact that the particularly chosen Hebraic word for love, this being *ahabah* as in the above verse (when David states that Jonathan's love to him was more wonderful than the love of women), always specifically refers to a *romantic* form of love – which allows us to see just how intimate

---

[29] As I SAMUEL 18:12-14 states during the very time of David's relationship with Jonathan:

> Now Saul was afraid of David, for the Lord was *with him* but had departed from [King] Saul...David was *acting wisely* in all his ways, for the Lord was *with* him.

this relationship really was in context to the entire story. The *ahabah* Hebrew translation for "love" herein in II SAMUEL 1:26 is the *same* rarely-used Hebrew word as found in GENESIS 29:20 regarding Jacob and Rachel's *romantic* relationship; I SAMUEL 20:17 which yet *again* repeats the *kind* of love that David and Jonathan specifically held for each other where it states "...BECAUSE OF HIS LOVE FOR HIM"; Amnon and Tamar in II SAMUEL 13:15 after *sexual intercourse* where it mentions the "...LOVE WITH WHICH HE HAD LOVED HER..."; and PROVERBS 5:19, specifically regarding *sex* between a man and his wife in its advice to

> ...REJOICE IN THE WIFE OF YOUR YOUTH...LET HER BREASTS SATISFY YOU AT ALL TIMES. BE EXHILARATED ALWAYS WITH HER LOVE.[30]

Again, all of these biblical passages use the very *same* Hebrew word for "love" specifically in regards to a *romantic*, sexually-borne *form* of love.[31] Yes, *including* the story of David and Jonathan.

The story of David and Jonathan's intimate, committed, and obviously sexually-charged love for one another has never been hidden in the Bible, so why should we now *pretend* that it is not there, or attempt to discredit it for what it *really* was...a love affair between two people of the same sex? To do so is to take

---

[30] PROVERBS 5:19
[31] See also Greenberg (as in n. 5 on page 57); Nissinen (as in n. 4 on page 83).

some parts of the Bible as our own, while ignoring the parts that do not neatly fit into our modern versions of religion, so-called "family values", and societal norms.

If Christ, as well as the rest of the Bible, supports homosexuality as a valid and legitimate reality of life, than who are *we* to pretend that this is not the case? The love between David and Jonathan, as well as between the Roman centurion and his partner, is the *same* kind of love that many now condemn in our places of worship, in many parts of the media in obscure ways, within our workplaces,[32] and inside many families where gay relatives are persecuted in all manners of mental and physical abuse ... and all of this in the current day and age, which is surprising, given that homosexuality has never before been such

---

[32] These same kind often also being the very ones who think nothing of bullying and victimizing their believing co-workers as well, and who treat women like the snakes they themselves are – even if the perpetrator is a woman *herself* – and neither corporate powers that be, nor the rest of the world, ever blinks twice at the daily hostile persecutions that go on in our offices today. But the treatment of these – as well as of our very own children – by such corporate snakes in suited clothing should become a high-profiled, much more publicly-denounced, and at times ultimately *imprisonable* offense due to the consequent heart attacks, strokes, mental breakdowns, and oft-times unbearable stresses directly caused towards both the individual recipient as well as to his or her family by such corporate bullies and health-destroying murderers if we have any hope of creating a more civilized society for our children to live in. Political correctness has not worked, and more often than not victimizes the victim and rewards the perpetrator. We are in a modern age, and must begin to *behave* like it.

an issue to be so shunned and condemned throughout mankind's history to the extent that it is now – despite what "political correctness" claims is the case in this brave new 21st Century. Maybe some just need to get a life.

If neither Christ, nor the early Christians, *ever* condemned a loving partnership between two people of the same sex, how can we call ourselves true "Christians" if we do the opposite? David and Jonathan were lovers. Their love was worthy enough to have been given attention in scripture. Today's God-loving gays and lesbians are worthy to be given positive attention, support, and understanding from us in like manner as true followers of God – as are those who have been torn and turned off to organized religion because of the prideful sins of those who "claim" to love God but who instead follow the ways of hell as the religious leaders of Christ's time did in their arrogant bigotry and diabolical self-righteousness. To be a spiritual stumbling block to gays and lesbians is to choose religious hypocrisy over and above the love of God, and to blindly follow after the traditions of man over the commandments of God.

6.3   Christ Warned Us *Against* Being Homophobic

Although homophobia was not as widespread amongst Roman and Greek cultures during the time of Christ as it is today throughout the world – as homosexuality was not "an issue" in those times, and was for the most part widely accepted as a normal part of life[33] – homophobia nonetheless still existed to a lesser degree. As such, Christ explicitly *condemned* any form of anti-gay speech coming from those – whether religious or not – who went around *hating,* judging, and condemning gay people.   In fact, he was so adamant and intolerant towards anyone who insulted another due to one's innate and God-given sexuality, that he stated that the repercussions of displaying such hatred were dire indeed from God's perspective. In affect, Christ actively *defended* the homosexuals of his time, as well as gays and lesbians of today, by his clear stance *against* any form of homophobic action, speech, or hate-crime.

In MATTHEW 5:22, Christ clearly states that we must not insult someone by calling him a *raca*. For

---

[33] In fact, homosexuality was widely practiced in ancient Mesopotamia, and there is no evidence that this was ever frowned upon by either society *or* the early Christians in general. See Vern L. Bullough, *Sexual Variance in Society and History.* University of Chicago Press, 1980; Gwendolyn Leick, *Sex and Eroticism in Mesopotamian Literature.* Routledge, 2003; and Raymond J. (as in n. 35 on page 73).

a long time, no one knew what this word meant, to where it now often shows up as an untranslated word in our modern bibles but which is usually noted as meaning "empty head", "good for nothing", or "you fool" – as scholars initially thought it might have been a derivative of the Hebrew *reqa*, which means the above.

But in 1934, an Egyptian papyrus dating back to 257 BC and written in Greek *contained* the word *rachas*, meaning *kinaidos* – or "faggot" as the closest parallel term in today's modern English slang. Many scholars now accept this to have been the true meaning of what Christ referred to as *raca* – thus making it clear that he was teaching against one being homophobic either through action or by one's spoken word.[34]

This makes a lot of sense if we consider the fact that *none* of Christ's followers who had known him during his earthly ministry *ever* mention anything derogatory about homosexuals or the subject of homosexuality in their writings... ever! Even Phillip himself never raised an issue when he met and explained the Gospel to the Ethiopian eunuch,[35] and wholeheartedly considered him to have become a gen-

---

[34] See also Warren Johansson, *Whosoever Shall Say to His Brother, Racha*. Volume 10, Cabirion, 1984; and Wayne Dynes, *Racha*. The Encyclopedia of Homosexuality edition. Garland, 1990.

[35] See note 7 on page 57.

uine and complete child of Christ without ever even lifting an eyelid regarding what his sexuality might or might not have been. Essentially, one's sexuality was never an issue in any way by the early Christians – thanks in part to Christ's having made clear, once and for all, that this is not an issue for God.

Modern-day religious zealots would do well to take note of this fact, and stop being – whether intentionally or not – stumbling blocks to gays and lesbians that they preach to and oftentimes outrightly condemn in one way or another. As it was with Christ and his early followers – as well as with early Christian history in the first centuries after Christ – so in like manner, modern Christianity must cease from making one's sexuality into some obscure "spiritual issue" – as it *never* was with them.

Likewise, if one's sexuality was *never* an issue with the very Son of God himself – or else he would surely have said so, which of course he never did in *any* way whatsoever – than it *must not* continue to be an issue for many of today's Christians. To do so is to go against both Christ and the Gospel to which he died and rose again for. May it never be.

6.4 Christ will Come Back for Gays and Lesbians

In LUKE 17:34-35 Christ mentions, in reference to the time immediately preceding his Second Coming to planet earth – specifically during what many would call *The Rapture*, where some will be taken up while still alive and enter God's kingdom without ever experiencing death, while those who have died throughout history and who are to be with God will likewise resurrect from their graves and join those who have been liberated from the bounds of earth – that:

> ...ON THAT NIGHT, THERE WILL BE TWO MEN IN ONE BED; ONE WILL BE TAKEN, AND THE OTHER WILL BE LEFT...TWO WOMEN GRINDING AT THE SAME PLACE; ONE WILL BE TAKEN, AND THE OTHER WILL BE LEFT.[36]

Consider this. Whether at the time in history in which Christ spoke these words, or even in modern times – just *how* likely would it be for two *adult* men to be found in one bed in the normal course of living life if they were not in some sort of relationship – and this considering virtually all cultures throughout the world without much of an exception? Could it be, considering not only the aforementioned points made from Christ's own statements and actions – and

---

[36] LUKE 17:34-35

with this additional phrase spoken almost in passing – again, that "...THERE WILL BE TWO MEN IN ONE BED..." – that he was trying to tell *us* – the modern age – something that society in his time took for granted due to homosexuality not having been the issue that it is today – but that modern Christianity (as well as most other religions) as an *organized* form of religion apart from true faith has *deliberately* ignored, condemned, and hidden itself from[37] – and this to the detriment of homosexual people, created and loved by God, who struggle to have a place in Christianity as well as in other faiths?

If Christ is coming back for gays and lesbians who have opened their door to God, modern Christianity would do well to begin to treat homosexuals not as outcasts and sinners, but as the fellow brothers and sisters in Christ who will reign with them eternally. For even the Old Testament states:

> FOR THUS SAYS THE LORD, "TO THE EUNUCHS WHO KEEP MY SABBATHS, AND CHOOSE WHAT PLEASES ME, AND HOLD FAST MY COVENANT; TO THEM I WILL GIVE IN MY HOUSE AND WITHIN MY WALLS A MEMORIAL, AND A NAME BETTER THAN THAT OF SONS AND DAUGHTERS; I WILL GIVE THEM AN EVERLASTING NAME WHICH WILL NOT BE CUT OFF." ISAIAH 56:4-5

---

[37] See also *Would Jesus Discriminate.* ⟨URL: http://www.wouldjesusdiscriminate.com⟩; and *Whosoever: An Online Magazine for Gay, Lesbian, Bisexual, and Transgender Christians.* ⟨URL: http://www.whosoever.org⟩.

To those who believe: Do we follow the commandments of God to love Him and our neighbor as we live
by faith and believe on the clear teachings of His Son
and *his* Word – or do we follow organized religion,
man-made tradition, and the choking deceptions of
pleasing mankind for the sake of our own fragile "reputations". For either we follow a Paulinian religion, or
the faith of Christ. So do not fear them, for God does
not make mistakes.

> YOU WHO FEAR THE LORD, WAIT FOR HIS MERCY;
> DO NOT STRAY, OR ELSE YOU MAY FALL. YOU
> WHO FEAR THE LORD, TRUST IN HIM, AND YOUR
> REWARD WILL NOT BE LOST. YOU WHO FEAR
> THE LORD, HOPE FOR GOOD THINGS, FOR LASTING
> JOY AND MERCY... HAS ANYONE TRUSTED IN THE
> LORD AND BEEN DISAPPOINTED? OR HAS ANYONE
> PERSEVERED IN THE FEAR OF THE LORD AND BEEN
> FORSAKEN? OR HAS ANYONE CALLED UPON HIM
> AND BEEN NEGLECTED? FOR THE LORD IS COMPAS-
> SIONATE AND MERCIFUL; HE FORGIVES SINS AND
> SAVES IN TIME OF DISTRESS. SIRACH 2:7-11

Chapter Seven

On Your Own Initiative

To use a mere two passages from Old Testament scripture, along with Paul's three verses of a potentially personal and biased viewpoint or outright misinterpretation, is to hypocritically excuse and attempt to hide overt and truly anti-Christian (and anti-scriptural) bigotry – especially when Christ is *telling* us to love one another (and ourselves for that matter) for who we are as individuals – as God has created each of us in *His* image to be – *regardless* of what one's sexual preferences might manifest itself as.

For many of those who believe, it all boils down to either a Paulinian-style of *religion* where the traditions of man silence and trump the teachings of God's Holy Spirit (whether or not Paul has had anything to do with it), which is essentially what much of Christian theology has in modern times unfortunately become – versus a genuine faith in Christ *that is separate from* organized religion, legalism, and man-made tradition, to where God's Holy Spirit is one's

teacher and leader[1] – which is what Christ himself
taught us as to how a true child-like and personal
faith that is fully dependant on one's Heavenly Father
alone (and not on religious dogma) must be. After
all, Christ did not die and rise again to give the
world *yet another* religion, but rather a personal and
direct relationship with God the Father as well as an
abundant life[2] ... plain and simple.

The *religiously-inclined* (as opposed to the *faith*-
based) often take sacred and life-affirming scripture
out of context and use it to justify their own precon-
ceived, self-benefiting, and face-saving ends – they
even justified slavery in this way during the American
slave trade using such things as Paul's writings in
I TIMOTHY 6:1-2[3] – whereas personal faith *listens* to

---

[1] See note 23 on page 33.

[2] As Christ stated:

> ... Very truly, I tell you, I am the gate for the sheep.
> All who came before me are thieves and bandits; but
> the sheep did not listen to them. I am the gate.
> Whoever enters by me will be saved, and will come
> in and go out and find pasture. The thief comes only
> to steal and kill and destroy. I came that they may
> have life, and have it *abundantly*. I am the good
> shepherd. I know my own and my own know me, just
> as the Father knows me and I know the Father. The
> good shepherd lays down his life for the sheep... I
> have power to lay it down, and I have power to take
> it up again. I have received this command from my
> Father. JOHN 10:7-18 [abridged].

[3] Though he *likely* never intended that his letters to *specific*
early congregations in *specific* circumstances be misinterpreted in

God and intuitively *knows* what is right and wrong, as Christ himself taught the world to do[4] – knowing that all that is love and good is of God, and all that is

such a manner by modern religious bullies. The same would likely apply to other non-spiritual issues and suggestions made by Paul – to where he is likely looking down on modern Christianity with great shame at how it has both taken literally as well as twisted his own words and opinions in order to develop *some* current-day ultra-fundamentalist styles of "Christianity" that we often see today. See also Frederick Douglass, *Narrative of the Life of Frederick Douglass, An American Slave: Written by Himself.* Yale University Press, 2001.

Furthermore, even the Quakers recognize this, to where they have rightly stated:

> What would Quakers say to people who point to teachings in the Bible against homosexuality? Most British Quakers, while finding much inspiration in the Bible, would not use it as the final or only authority. We believe in obedience to the same Spirit of God that inspired the writers of the Bible and that we feel can speak directly to people today.

> We remember that the writers of the New Testament accepted the institution of slavery but Christians no longer keep slaves. Parts of the New Testament seem to support the argument against the ordination of women but several churches now ordain women. How the Christian Church decides which of the teachings in the Bible are eternal and which were 'of their time' is an important issue. Quakers, *Quaker Views - Close Relationships*. Quaker Life, 2008.

[4] As Christ stated:

> When you see a cloud rising in the West, immediately you say, "a shower is coming", and so it turns out. And when you see a south wind blowing, you say "it will be a hot day", and it turns out that way. You hypocrites! You know how to analyze the appearance of the earth and the sky, but why do you not analyze

malicious and oppressive is of the evil one. . . these the very same things that breed hatred towards the poor in spirit[5] and segregations of all sorts.[6]

Consider the gay or lesbian couple that you know or have heard about, for instance. If they love one another – as a parent loves her child; as a young heterosexual couple is inseparable; and as an elderly couple on a sinking ship is loyal and true to one another until the bitter end – yes, even to the point of going down with the ship together[7] – *that* form of

this present time? And why do you not even *on your own initiative* judge what is right? LUKE 12:54-57

[5] As Christ stated in the famous Sermon on the Mount:

Blessed are the poor in spirit, for theirs is the kingdom of heaven." MATTHEW 5:3.

Please note that the phrase "poor in spirit" literally translates from the Greek as "those who are not spiritually arrogant" – or the "humble in spirit" – as referenced from the NASB within this verse as per the LockmanFoundation, editor, *Updated New American Standard Bible*. Zondervan Publishing House, 1999.

[6] See also Jack Rogers, *Jesus, the Bible, and Homosexuality: Explode the Myths, Heal the Church*. Westminster John Knox Press, 2006.

[7] As excellently portrayed by an elderly couple who decide to remain in their sinking ship's cabin in a loving embrace as they lay in bed together – and this while the rest of the world is panicking and falling apart around them in James Cameron, *Titanic*. 20th Century Fox;Paramount Pictures;Lightstorm Entertainment, 1997.

genuine and faithful love *must be* from God. For such love cannot exist *apart* from God.[8] For God *is* love.[9]

All that is good *is* of God. Thus do not let them use religion as an excuse – as the Pharisees and teachers of the law did in the time of Christ – as they likewise do today.[10] To judge and condemn the love between two men or two women – whom God has created and joined together – is to judge and condemn God *Himself* – and thus to *question* His own judgment, and to *mock His* own creation and work.[11] To condemn the

---

[8] As once rightly stated by the British Quakers:

> Where there is a genuine tenderness, an openness to responsibility, and the seed of commitment, God is surely not shut out. Can we not say that God can enter any relationship in which there is a measure of selfless love? British Quakers, *Towards a Quaker View of Sex*. Quaker Home Service, 1998.

[9] As the apostle John, who wrote both the GOSPEL OF JOHN as well as the BOOK OF REVELATIONS, writes in one of three letters to the early Christians, particularly in I JOHN 4:7-8:

> Dear friends, let us love one another, for love comes from God. Everyone who loves has been born of God and knows God. Whoever does not love does not know God, because God *is* love.

[10] See also Brannum-Harris (as in n. 21 on page 65).

[11] Even as some Quakers have rightly said,

> We affirm the love of God for all people, whatever their sexual orientation, and our conviction that sexuality is an important part of human beings as created by God, so that to reject people on the grounds of their sexual behavior is a denial of God's creation. Quakers of Westminster Meeting, *statement from*. Quakers, 1963.

expression of such love is to condemn the self, and the intelligence that God has given to each one of us in more than adequate sufficiency.

Hypothetically speaking, even *if* Paul had for some reason been homophobic – which seems *extremely* unlikely when considering the rest of his vast body of written works where there is no mention of anything that directly referred to homosexuality as we know it today apart from what has already been examined in Chapter 4, while also giving consideration for his widespread statements about the importance of both love and faith as the foundations of the Christian walk[12] – it would likely have been due to his self-admitting over-zealous Judaic past from both a traditional as well as orthodox perspective,[13] and clearly *not* due to anything Christ – nor any of his apostles (*or* disciples for that matter) – had *ever* said, written, or expressed – as we have clearly seen throughout this work. Nevertheless, from all that we have looked at, Paul was *not* homophobic in any way whatsoever, and seems to have actually *defended* innocent gays and lesbians by speaking out against

---

[12] See note 35 on page 52.

[13] Paul himself admits this when he states:

> I advanced in Judaism beyond many among my people of the same age, for I was far more zealous for the traditions of my ancestors. GALATIANS 1:14

the kidnapping of homosexuals for purposes of feeding the sex slave trade, in addition to condemning the ritualistic practices involving regular violent rapes performed against shrine prostitutes by both male and female participants – in particular those trapped within the widespread Roman Cybelean Cult of that time, including other pagan cults like it – as has been seen in Chapter 4.

But for the sake of argument to those who care – even in the *unlikely* event that Paul actually did mean to speak against homosexuality in and of itself in a mere three scattered verses aforementioned out of hundreds that he wrote, who would *you* choose to believe – to follow – Christ, or Paul? Who is attributed as the *Living* Word of God – Christ, or Paul?[14] Who is your ultimate spiritual teacher – if you are a believer? Who speaks to you through your intuition when you stand still for a while and begin to listen – Christ's Holy Spirit who he promised he would send and who would teach us all things and bring to our remembrance all that He had taught us,[15] or Paul's words? Does a Christian worship Christ, or Paul? Does he or she depend on the words of Christ and the guidance of God's Spirit over and above man's speculations, or on a Paulinian structure of opinion? Does one live by faith, or by the many conflicting

---

[14] See Appendix C, sub-section C.5 on page 221.
[15] See note 23 on page 33.

voices one hears every day from an infinite number of
sources? Who truly *is* the Way – the Son of the Living
God who taught us about truth, love, and solidity of
mind – or the traditions of man, and the vast opinions
they carry and load us all with if we so let them?
Should a Jew follow God by faith, or the law by works?
Even Paul *himself* said by faith, and faith *alone* – did
he not?[16]

If Christ *did* indeed categorically state that some
are *meant* to be born, and thereby live as, homosexuals – as has been thoroughly discussed in Chapter 5
on page 77 – than who will *you* choose to believe – to
follow – Christ, or modern-day organized religion? On
your own initiative you *can* judge what is right. . . as
Christ taught us to do.[17]

Christ himself stated that we are not to call anyone on earth our teacher – for it is *His* Holy Spirit
who we must listen to above all else[18] – even above
Epistolic letters whether written by Paul or whomever
it might be. His Spirit *supersedes* anything written by man, and we must accept this if we are to
be affective followers of Christ who genuinely walk
in love and who bear much fruit[19] without getting

---

[16] See note 18 on page 42.

[17] As quoted in note 4 on page 127.

[18] See note 23 on page 33.

[19] As Christ said:

> . . . every scribe who has become a disciple of the
> kingdom of heaven is like a head of a household,

bogged down in religious legalism and vain theology
– lest we become immovable, stubborn, and stiff-
necked stumbling blocks to the desperate-hearted as
well as towards *millions* who are seeking a new life
of spiritual freedom and mental tranquility while we
wrongly continue to tell them that they must change
who they have always been from birth. May it never
be!

I often state that one should try to, at least *once*
in a lifetime – if not more – perform an experiment
and read *only* what Jesus Christ stated throughout
the Gospels (these being the books of MATTHEW, MARK,
LUKE, and JOHN in the New Testament portion of the
Bible) *all the way* through – Christ's words often being
marked in red letters in many versions – and see
what one might get out of such an exercise. If this
is done in spirit and in truth, one will certainly look
on homosexuality – amongst *many* other things – in
a *totally* different light than how organized religion
has portrayed it in modern times! Try it for yourself –
I promise you'll be pleasantly surprised... I stake my
name on it.

Thus to use a mere five ambiguous verses in
the *entire* Judeo-Christian Bible out of context to
attempt to *wrongly* condemn gays and lesbians, while

who brings out of his treasure things new and old.
MATTHEW 13:52.

deliberately ignoring the many specific Biblical passages that seem to actually *support* homosexuality
either directly or by inference – is to deliberately
lie to the masses in order to satisfy and deceptively
justify one's own homophobic and legalistic agendas
– and to thereby become a stumbling block towards
homosexuals wishing to have a personal relationship
with their loving God...which is a much *greater* sin
than anything to do with sexual behavior of any kind
– gay *or* straight.

   After all, sex is a basic and vital form of human expression, as well as a vehicle for creativity, emotional
healing, mental well-being, spiritual awakening, and
much-needed physical exercise given to us by God. So
who are *we* to dictate how others should manifest it
when those involved have a genuine mutual respect
towards one another?   There are more important
things in life.   We need to get over it and start
loving souls instead of repelling them away from the
very God who loves them and who wants nothing
more than to be their life-long and eternal First Love,
protector, defender, and confidant.   Who are *we* to
stand in God's way...and to thwart the gift of self-
expression that He has given us.

   Thus if you are Jewish or Christian as well as
being – or suspect yourself as being – gay or lesbian,
know and be confident that your scriptures affirm and
support you as you have been created to be. Therefore,

to the Jewish and Christian gay people of the world –
your scriptures, and the foundations of your religion,
wholeheartedly *support* who you are – no matter *what*
the ignorantly-naïve few – who cannot be bothered to
educate themselves on these matters – might or might
not say.

As Christ said in LUKE 12:57,

> AND WHY DO YOU NOT EVEN ON YOUR OWN INITIA-
> TIVE JUDGE WHAT IS RIGHT?[20]

He did *not* say on the merits of a religion, a doctrine, a
preacher, a national policy, a community, or a cultural
idiosyncrasy – but on *your own* initiative – on the use
of *common sense*, influenced by nothing more than
love, justice, mercy,[21] and by God's guidance through
His Spirit of Truth (or Holy Spirit) that has been
spoken of in this work...this guidance which comes
by sincere prayer and listening to *His* voice above all
others.

---

[20] See also note 4 on page 127.

[21] As Christ told the religious leaders who themselves were
driven by political spin and religious traditions and enchainments
of every kind – as opposed to by the intimate voice of God through
a personal, genuine, and direct relationship *with* Him:

> Woe to you, scribes and Pharisees, hypocrites! For
> you tithe mint and dill and cummin [performing
> aspects of *religiosity*], and have neglected the
> weightier provisions of the law: justice and mercy
> and faithfulness. MATTHEW 23:23.

Do not let organized religion tear you apart... and do not be deprived of what God has created and intended for your *own* life. To do so is to become *like them* – and soon your love grows cold, and your purpose defiled beyond recognition. And do not hinder those whom God has created in *His* likeness – for to do so is to hinder Christ himself in the name of religion... and to inevitably become a stumbling block to those who are coming to God in spirit and in truth through the faith of a child.

If God does not condemn you, than how can man? If God is for us, who can be against us?[22] Keep your eyes on *Him* alone, and not on organized religion. Put your trust in *Him*, and *not* on the ever-wavering mood swings of mankind, nor on opinionated dogma – whether from preachers, teachers, texts – nor even on this very book. Speak to Christ *directly*. You don't *need* religion for that. And listen to *His* voice – in spirit and in truth... and you will *never* go wrong.

DON'T LET THEM HINDER YOUR SOUL

---

[22] As Paul himself stated:

What then shall we say to these things? If God is for us, who is against us? ... Who will bring a charge against God's elect? God is the one who justifies; who is the one who condemns? Who will separate us from the love of Christ? ROMANS 8:31-35 [abridged].

Chapter Eight

Enjoy God – Without Over-Analysis or Dilemmas

If you have been enriched by anything from my experience and what is attested to herein, than I have accomplished my goal in encouraging faith *without* the needless and time-wasting imprisonment of "organized religion"... the historic *stumbling block* to God and all that *is* of God. At the very least, I would hope – for those who have struggled with the issue of homosexuality as it relates to faith – irrespective of one's own sexual preference – that this work has encouraged a more Christ-like approach that does not vilify the millions throughout the world who are *also* genuine children of God – namely gay and lesbian people who either yearn to, or who have *already* come to Christ not by being religious *nor* through organized religion, but in spirit and in truth. Either way, it is better that one be tolerant, and make a sincere effort at comprehending accurate biblical interpretation on this topic, than to be some sort of a traditionally-blinded and religiously-motivated stumbling block to the many who sincerely seek after God but who cannot find Him due to the widespread, deceptive, and erroneous preconceptions about this subject as it relates to biblical study in this brave new world that deprives them of spiritual freedom and mental rest.

But above all else, I hope that the reader bear in mind that God calls *all* of mankind to Himself, and that if you answer His call, you do not have to become *like* the modern-day religious zealot to be his child. Seek Him from within the sacred privacy of your heart and you *will* find Him – seek Him from an organized and religiosity-tainted platform and you will more often than not find contradiction, confusion, and manipulations.[1] Thus, for those that seek Him – find Him by beginning to speak to Him *directly* and on your own initiative and free will – talk to Him in faith, knowing that He *will* listen and *will* reveal Himself to those that come to Him with a willing and open heart and spirit – to those who sincerely seek for Truth in a world where love is lost.

Enter into His presence in *whatever* way He leads you. Enjoy it! And don't over-analyze and complicate. If you wish, open a Bible and read the four gospels of MATTHEW, MARK, LUKE, and JOHN. And pay especially close attention to the words of Christ. What he has to

---

[1] Though not all religious organizations are like this, as is thoroughly explained in Appendix B on page 187.

say will surprise you for sure! In *every* positive sense. Don't delve any deeper than is necessary, just take these four books in.

Maybe later – much, much, later on – *if* it so suits you, you might decide to find a church[2] or group that *accepts you* for who you are as God has Himself created you to be – and who will not desecrate your relationship with Him through misinformation, rule, ambiguity, slander, hypocrisy, misplaced guilt, shame, and fear. This is totally up to you... and is a decision made *exclusively* by yourself and with the guidance of God's Spirit. Let *Him* lead you, and no one else.

And if and when you *do* decide to delve into the remainder of the Old or New Testament – *if* you so desire – do so with the awareness that it must be taken in context, considering the time of writing, who was writing, and to whom it was being written to. Christ's words in the aforementioned Gospels are far weightier, more powerful, and more revealing than probably anything you will *ever* read on earth... and I am personally content with that.

As having been previously explained in great detail, Christ has promised us that *His* Spirit of Truth would personally and individually reveal to us *all things* as we sincerely listen to His voice, and as

---

[2] See advise on going about finding a church – if you ever decide to on your own *free* will – that reflects Christ's teachings and unconditional love for you in Appendix B on page 187.

we continually and straightforwardly ask God for
guidance – so don't supersede what the Spirit of
God tells you with the external words, doctrines, and
traditions of man. And never, *ever*, lose the God-given
fearless confidence[3] that He has *already* given to you
(all you have to do is *use* it) – and which He wants you
to always live by. For He is within *all* who open their
door to Him *without any* preconditions or exceptions –
and He will *never* let you go.[4]

Lastly, neither let the trials and tribulations of
life, nor the religious, snatch your faith away from
your heart – remember Christ's parable of the Sower
and the Seed? Don't deprive yourself the joy, peace,
enjoyment, and clarity of talking to and *knowing* God,
His perfect and rewarding guidance for your life, and
His unconditional and eternal love for you – not on

---

[3] As Christ rightly said:

These things I have spoken to you, so that in Me you
may have peace. In the world you have tribulation,
but take courage; I have overcome the world. JOHN
16:33 ... Do not let your heart be troubled, nor let it
be fearful. JOHN 14:27

[4] Jesus explained to us that,

My sheep listen to my voice; I know them, and
they follow me. I give them eternal life, and they
shall *never* perish; and *no one* can snatch them out
of my hand. My Father, who has given them to me,
is *greater than all*; and *no one* is able to snatch them
out of my Father's hand. I and the Father are one.
JOHN 10:27-30

their account – for the kingdom of God *belongs* to you for the taking...just as you are.

My Child,

You may not know me, but I know everything about you.

PSALM 139:1

I know when you sit down and when you rise up.

PSALM 139:2

I am familiar with all your ways.

PSALM 139:3

Even the very hairs on your head are numbered.

MATTHEW 10:29-31

For you were made in my image.

GENESIS 1:27

In me you live and move and have your being.

ACTS 17:28

For you are my offspring.

ACTS 17:28

I knew you even before you were conceived.

JEREMIAH 1:4-5

I chose you when I planned creation.

EPHESIANS 1:11-12

You were not a mistake, for all your days are written
in my book.

PSALM 139:15-16

I determined the exact time of your birth and where
you would live.

ACTS 17:26

You are fearfully and wonderfully made.

PSALM 139:14

I knit you together in your mother's womb.

PSALM 139:13

And brought you forth on the day you were born.

PSALM 71:6

I have been misrepresented by those who don't know
me.

JOHN 8:41-44

I am not distant and angry, but am the complete
expression of love.

1 JOHN 4:16

And it is my desire to lavish my love on you.

1 JOHN 3:1

Simply because you are my child and I am your
Father.

1 JOHN 3:1

I offer you more than your earthly father ever could.

MATTHEW 7:11

For I am the perfect father.

MATTHEW 5:48

Every good gift that you receive comes from my hand.

JAMES 1:17

For I am your provider and I meet all your needs.

MATTHEW 6:31-33

My plan for your future has always been filled with hope.

JEREMIAH 29:11

Because I love you with an everlasting love.

JEREMIAH 31:3

My thoughts toward you are countless as the sand on the seashore.

PSALMS 139:17-18

And I rejoice over you with singing.

ZEPHANIAH 3:17

I will never stop doing good to you.

JEREMIAH 32:40

For you are my treasured possession.

EXODUS 19:5

I desire to establish you with all my heart and all my soul.

JEREMIAH 32:41

And I want to show you great and marvelous things.

JEREMIAH 33:3

If you seek me with all your heart, you will find me.

DEUTERONOMY 4:29

Delight in me and I will give you the desires of your heart.

PSALM 37:4

For it is I who gave you those desires.

PHILIPPIANS 2:13

I am able to do more for you than you could possibly imagine.

EPHESIANS 3:20

For I am your greatest encourager.

II THESSALONIANS 2:16-17

I am also the Father who comforts you in all your troubles.

II CORINTHIANS 1:3-4

When you are brokenhearted, I am close to you.

PSALM 34:18

As a shepherd carries a lamb, I have carried you close to my heart.

ISAIAH 40:11

One day I will wipe away every tear from your eyes.

REVELATION 21:3-4

And I'll take away all the pain you have suffered on this earth.

REVELATION 21:3-4

I am your Father, and I love you even as I love my
son, Jesus.

JOHN 17:23

For in Jesus, my love for you is revealed.

JOHN 17:26

He is the exact representation of my being.

HEBREWS 1:3

He came to demonstrate that I am for you, not
against you.

ROMANS 8:31

And to tell you that I am not counting your sins.

II CORINTHIANS 5:18-19

Jesus died so that you and I could be reconciled.

II CORINTHIANS 5:18-19

His death was the ultimate expression of my love for
you.

I JOHN 4:10

I gave up everything I loved that I might gain your
love.

ROMANS 8:31-32

If you receive the gift of my son Jesus, you receive me.

I JOHN 2:23

And nothing will ever separate you from my love
again.

ROMANS 8:38-39

Come home and I'll throw the biggest party heaven
has ever seen.

Luke 15:7

I have always been Father, and will always be Father.

Ephesians 3:14-15

My question is... Will you be my child?

John 1:12-13

I am waiting for you.

Luke 15:11-32

Love, Your Dad Almighty God[5]

---

[5] Father's Love Letter: An Intimate Message From God To
You. Father's Love Letter used by permission Father Heart Com-
munications Copyright 1999-2011 www.FathersLoveLetter.com

Part I

Appendices

Appendix A

Heterosexuals are People Too

This section deals with premarital sex, as well as other incidentally-related topics as well. Although a Christian-based analysis continues to be employed herein, the arguments are applicable to all other major religious backgrounds – especially since the majority of which take a similar stance on the subject as the modern-day version of Christianity. That being said, let us begin.

A.1 What *is* Adultery, Really?

Adultery is defined as "the voluntary sexual intercourse between a *married* person and someone other than his or her lawful spouse."[1] As such, it has *nothing whatsoever* to do with premarital sex, whether gay or straight. To define it any other way is misleading – as many within organized religion have done. Furthermore, to state that premarital sex – when those involved are not married to anyone else – relates in any way to "adultery" is to become a stumbling block to those who are in fact *not* committing adultery – and to therefore load many with unbearable burdens of guilt and shame that only organized religion – apart from God – does so well. To do so is to be a stumbling block between sexually-active heterosexual people and the true and liberating faith that has been freely given to all of humanity through Christ.

It is understandable why Jesus explicitly mentioned the issue of sexual chastity *only once* in his ministry – and this strictly within the *context* of adultery – which, again is defined as having sexual relations with one who is *already* married and who is *not* one's spouse.   Christ stated that adultery is a legitimate reason for divorce – as we can see from his referring to "marital unfaithfulness" when he talked about divorce in MATTHEW 5:32[2] – though within the context of his having referred to adultery

---

[1]As rightly put from Webster, *Webster's New Universal Unabridged Dictionary*. Barnes & Noble Books, 1992.

[2] As he states:

> ...but I say to you that everyone who divorces [or "sends away"] his wife, except for the cause of

on *other* occasions, he interestingly spoke of the act of adultery as *leaving* or *abandoning* one's spouse, as opposed to whether or not extra-marital sex may or may not be involved in the decision to divorce – so that, in the case of marital unfaithfulness, it is primarily the act of *abandonment*, and *not* the subject of sex in and of itself, that may be the real issue in his looking unfavorably against other reasons for divorcing – as God is in the business of building relationships, not tearing them down. Of course, that being said, common sense – given to us by God – would state that persistent physical abuse within a marriage would also be a legitimate reason for divorce – especially as this in itself can be seen as the abuser having already *abandoned* or *separated* from the abused spouse simply by the continuous act of violence – thus fitting into Christ's own focused definition of adultery as being *more so* the act of abandonment, due to his not having dwelt on extra-marital sex as the primary focus on this subject.

---

unchastity [or "marital unfaithfulness"], makes her commit adultery... MATTHEW 5:32.

It is interesting to note that the term "sends away" is used herein. As such, the act of divorce can in itself be considered adultery – even though no sex may be involved – thus re-enforcing the idea that, in Christ's words, adultery does not refer to one's simply having had sex with another without one's spouse's consent – to where adultery can be considered as being the act of divorcing – or abandoning, or "sending away" – one's spouse... irrespective of whether or not any extra-marital sex is involved or not.

So adultery refers directly to either the abandonment of a marriage – which does *not* in itself require any sexual act having been done by anyone involved – or cheating on one's spouse, especially if done *without* mutual consent or agreement between spouses. The reason "consent" is used herein is because polygamy – being married to multiple spouses at the same time – never seems to have been "outlawed" in the Judeo-Christian Bible[3] – neither in the Old nor New Testament scriptures. But whatever one's stance may be, the point is – by Christ's very own definition – adultery *always* involves a *marriage* – plain and simple. Whether or not extra-marital sex in and of itself is part of it or not seems only *incidental* to what adultery is conventionally defined as – again, his definition having been focused primarily on the act of abandoning one's spouse – irrespective of whether or not an extra-marital sexual affair exists or not. This obviously does not include single people having premarital sex in any way whatsoever, and organized religion must stop inferring that it does, lest it continue to turn the world off to the Gospel by its fanatical preaching against a sort of sex that in truth does *not* in fact involve any participant who is married to someone else.

---

[3] See note 2 on page 152.

A.2   Pre-marital Sex is *not* an Issue

So now that we have clarified what adultery actually *is*, and having noted that premarital sex has nothing whatever to do with it, let us now look into the subject of sex between people who are *not* married to anyone else. So therefore, in regards to sex *outside* of marriage (or premarital sex where no one involved is married to anyone else) – such as gay, lesbian, and premarital heterosexual sex – it would seem that Christ was *completely silent* on these specific issues[4] apart from what has already been discussed in this book – to where if sex outside of marriage was such a "big deal" to the God who created sexual desire in the first place, Christ *surely* would have repeatedly and clearly mentioned this – as he did other issues to do with inter-human relationships. Furthermore, it is also interesting to note that not even his apostles, nor anybody else in either the Old or New Testaments,

---

[4] Yes, Christ does indeed seem to state that some people are *meant* to be gay from birth, and therefore not meant to marry – thus making it clear that homosexuality (gay or lesbian) is a part of God's plan for some, and must therefore not be condemned by those claiming to desire to do God's will – despite what religious tradition and organized religions of most varieties wrongly claim out of either self-righteous hypocrisy, ignorance of what scripture really says about the subject, outright deception when one has been made aware of the true biblical stance on this, or repression-borne homophobia. See this book's main matter for an extensive discussion on this topic.

every explicitly and clearly speak against premarital sex whatsoever.

In addition to this very vital point, please also note that the phrase "sexual immorality" in both MATTHEW 15:19 and MARK 7:21[5] (same day, same context of conversation, different Gospels) is sometimes *erroneously* translated by modern contemporaries into the word "fornication" – the phrase "sexual immorality" having been used therein along with other short-listed terms when Christ was trying to explain things that "defile a man" (such as murder, theft, envy, slander, and arrogance). This phrase, as used in the cited verses, comes from the Greek word *porneia*, which is in turn derived from the word *porneuo* – which though by direct translation does in fact mean "sexual immorality" – it more often than not refers

---

[5] Furthermore, another word that was used in Mark 7:5-23 was *sensuality* – the Greek word *aselgeia* essentially referring to lawless excess, such as the squandering love for and dedication to luxuries and wealth before the love of God and one's fellow man; and also translatable as *unrestrained* lawlessness or unrestrained vice, such as in the love of violence or any form of crime against another, as well as limitless vice (such as alcoholism or drug *abuse* – or whatever it might be that is done excessively without moderation – as Christ himself stated that we should not be *weighed down* with dissipation, drunkenness, and the worries of life in LUKE 21:34) – and thus not necessarily how this word is commonly thought of today as *exclusively* referring to sex in and of itself. Furthermore, Christ also stated herein that it is *not* what comes *into* the mouth that makes one "unclean" – but rather what comes out of the heart.

particularly to how some versions correctly translate it as – that being *whoredom* or *prostitution*.

Furthermore, *porneuo* comes from the Greek word *porne*, which literally refers to a female prostitute.[6] Most importantly, the word *fornication*, as used in modern times, has wrongly been imposed a rather *contemporary* meaning – the word itself only having been in existence and used in recent centuries, to where by modern implication is commonly (but erroneously) *assumed* to mean premarital sex – even though the word never even *existed* before the 14th century when it was first used in the Middle English as derived from the Latin word *fornix* – meaning *vault*, an *arch*, and *brothel* – the derivative *fornix* referring specifically to a vaulted arch where prostitutes used to come together in Roman times to market their trade.[7]

Furthermore, the additional derivative *fornices* referred specifically to such arches, having been understood in said Roman times to mean *brothels* – thus prostitutes selling their services "under the arches" so-to-speak. As such, from its original use centuries ago post the 14th century, the word *fornication* seems only to refer to sex involving prostitution, and therefore having *nothing* at all to do with sexual activity or

---

[6] Foundation (as in n. 23 on page 46), p.1559.

[7] See also T. F. Hoad, editor, *The Concise Oxford Dictionary of English Etymology*. Oxford University Press, 1993.

behavior between two consenting, unmarried adults
(be they heterosexual *or* homosexual). In addition
to this, no such word (*fornication*, that is) – nor any
similar variant – ever even *existed* in the time of
Christ – so that to *wrongly* attempt to force upon a
translation of the Greek *porneia* as supposing to mean
our *modernized* equivalent of *fornication* – with its
own definition as referring to sex between unmarried
people – is to simply put a word into Christ's mouth
that he did *not* say – especially when what he most
likely was referring to was sexual activity *involving*
prostitution in the first instance as stated, and possibly to rape, incest, the worship of idols through sexual
ritualistic practices, and possibly even to bestiality
(sex with animals) – as will be further explained
herein.

Hence, these were the common things that cultures of the time would likely have thought of when
hearing such a term, when taking both Old and New
Testament writings that also use the phrase in both
Hebraic and Greek versions of the same into account,
as well as on considering cultural context and meaning at the time[8] – to where in reality the word *porneia*
(as used by Christ) does *not* in fact seem to mean
either premarital or any other form of "conventional"

---

[8] See also the excellent book Philo Thelos, *Divine Sex:
Liberating Sex from Religious Tradition*. Trafford Publishing,
2006.

sex (again, either gay or straight sex) – and as such neither *porneia* nor *fornication* should erroneously be *assumed* to mean general sexual behavior between consenting and unmarried adults (which many lightly suppose it to mean in this day and age). To do so is to not only inaccurately translate a phrase to fit our modern way of thinking about sex in general by modern man, but also to *presume* and impose upon Christ a modern definition which was not necessarily being referred to – neither explicitly nor implicitly. In other words, it would seem that Christ *never* explicitly said that premarital sex is wrong in and of itself. In fact, *nothing* of the sort is ever explicitly claimed by him in any manner whatsoever – contrary to what many major organized religions of today state as based on their *own* devised man-made traditions and taboos.

Prominent biblical scholars and translators *clearly* make this differentiation as well – that the word *porneia* used herein refers to either "sexual immorality" in general, or prostitution – and therefore *not* particularly to either premarital nor gay sex – as seen in all the reliable and widely regarded biblical translations of today[9] – either in footnotes referring

---

[9] Such Bible versions including:

- The New American Standard
- New Revised Standard Version
  [continued on the next page]

to the same phrase, or in direct translations *not* as "fornication", but rather as either "sexual immorality" or "whoredom"...in other words, prostitution. So when sister Eunice or aunt Tabatha shove this verse in your face and erroneously claim that the original translation meant "fornication" as interpreted into our skewed definition of premarital sex today, you can now show them this book along with a nice glass of whiskey to absorb the shock that they will surely experience from years of believing everything their priest, rabbi, or self-proclaimed guru has fervently, fanatically, and erroneously claimed via religious tradition and the all-too-deceptive casual claims that originate from social taboo, political correctness, and "moral majority rule".

Furthermore, even Paul *himself*, in I CORINTHIANS 5:1, used the same word – *porneia* – to refer to a case of *incest*; and Christ used it in reference to *adultery* and how divorce fits into it in MATTHEW 5:32 and 19:9; while ACTS 15:20, 15:29, and 21:25 uses it in the context of what seems to be sexual rituals during the worship of idols – as has been seen throughout this

- Updated New American Standard Bible
- New International Version
- Hebrew Names Version
- Young's Literal Translation
- International Standard Version

work as having been common practice in the pagan-influenced Roman times. So it seems as though even Paul *himself* – when using the word *pornos* (which is derived from *porne* and meaning a *male* prostitute)[10] in I CORINTHIANS 6:9 and again in HEBREWS 13:4 – did *not* intend for this to mean "fornication" – or premarital sex. In short, Christ himself seems to *never* have explicitly stated that either premarital sex in and of itself was in any way against God – which would lead us to conclude that the use of the word *porneia* in MATTHEW 15:9 and MARK 7:21 was referring either *only* to prostitution; or *possibly* to prostitution, rape, incest, bestiality, and sexual rituals in idol worship when considering linguistic history as well as context of cultural and normative use of the term at the time.

A.3   God Cares More About the Soul Rather than About One's Sex Life

This having been thoroughly explained, one must also remember – in regards to prostitution itself – that Christ was well known to have *associated with* and *loved* – in a non-sexual manner, of course – the prostitutes of his time who came to him, to the point where he even stated that they were entering into

---

[10] Foundation (as in n. 23 on page 46), p. 1559.

the Kingdom of God *before* the religious hypocrites in his midst because these prostitutes (as well as tax collectors, and "sinners" in general) had believed. In other words, they had placed their trust[11] on him, and thereby in God the Father.[12] As such, he made clear to all that God does not *care* as much about one's private sexual life as He does about one's soul, well-being, and happiness – so long as one is respecting, and thereby loving by one's actions and attitudes – oneself, one's sexual partner (temporary or otherwise), and whomever *else* may be involved on an emotional level within the circle of our more physical intimacies.

As such, I would surmise – by the things that Christ stated, as well as by what he did *not* make a big deal out of – that God is again *much* more concerned about the *spiritual* health of the individual as well as about one's willingness to open ones door to *Him* with the faith of a child – than in one's personal sex life. Jesus seems to have made this abundantly clear in his words, actions, and by his own life-long example. Hence, in comparison to a relationship with one's Creator, sex is a *non-issue* with God.

As such, don't allow someone to tell you that God is not with you, nor for you, just because of your sex life or lifestyle when you are not causing harm to either yourself or your partner – and are respecting *both*

---

[11] See note 23 on page 45.
[12] MATTHEW 21:31-32

yourself and all those involved in the process...hence loving your neighbor in action by respecting personal limits, not breaking up relationships, and not physically or emotionally harming someone else. God *created* sex – don't let them take that gift away from you – and don't let them make you doubt your relationship with God just because your sex life might be somewhat *different* from theirs – especially when you are considering God's guidance in the process. Be tolerant towards others' views on sexuality – but don't let others make you stumble in your relationship with God because of *their* own hang-ups, prejudices, and ignorance.

A.4   Beauty is *Meant* to be Appreciated

Another topic that people oftentimes take issue with relates to such things as pornography, voyeurism, visual appreciation, or simply fantasizing on the beauty of another. They will, especially amongst major religious circles, claim that involving oneself in such things amounts to sin – often wrongly citing Christ when he was teaching on the Ten Commandments as he showed us that sin begins in the heart – though he himself never explicitly stated that either *fantasizing* or doing any of the above in and of themselves are in any way wrong – but rather that it is the overly-

excessive and addictive use of *anything* – be it alcohol, drugs, work, religiosity, porn, worry, fear, or whatever else that one can form a solid addiction to in the place of a healthy relationship with God, the self, and others – that is the issue.[13]

Many stuck on traditional aspects of organized religion will somehow magically conclude that, on Christ's stating that to look at a woman to lust for her[14] as being tantamount to *adultery* of the heart

---

[13] See note 5 on page 156.

[14] Christ seemed *not* to be talking about fantasizing or thinking sexual thoughts at all (which of course are God-given processes of desire and need for fulfillment in our own nature as He has created and intended both for procreation as well as enjoyment) – but rather about earnestly wishing for, or *coveting*, another's spouse instead when he stated:

> You have heard that it was said, "YOU SHALL NOT COMMIT ADULTERY"; but I say to you, that everyone who looks on a woman to lust [the Greek word for "lust" herein being *epithumeo* – which means to "earnestly desire" *and* "covet" something (or someone) *belonging to* someone else] for her has committed adultery [sex with one who is currently *married*] with her already in his heart. MATTHEW 5:27-28.

Again, the use of *epithumeo* (translated as "to lust" in English translations) means "to covet" in the Greek (translated from the Aramaic language Christ spoke) – which makes more sense in context as Christ is teaching on *both* the seventh of the Ten Commandments regarding *adultery* (DEUTERONOMY 5:18) – as well as on the tenth commandment which states that one must not *covet* a neighbor's wife (DEUTERONOMY 5:21) – which is also being implicitly referred to simply by the use of the Greek word *epithumeo* – "to covet". Essentially, he is telling us that sin begins in the heart, so that it is merely enough to earnestly desire to *have* one's neighbor's wife to commit adultery – this

– again *notice* the word *adultery* – that such things
as pornography, fantasizing, voyeurism, premarital
sex, and the rest of it must be included in what he
was talking about. Yet many now believe he was
not speaking of the aforementioned at all, but was
rather *specifically* referring to the act of *coveting* with
the intent to *pursue* the spouse of another for one's
own possession or use – plain and simple. After all,
Christ *did* make clear that what he was specifically
speaking about was *adultery*, and not erotic thoughts
or fantasies in and of themselves when taken into context with the fact that he was talking in reference to
both the commandments *against* adultery as well as
coveting what belongs to someone else by the original
manuscripts' use of the Greek word *epithumeo* – which
can both mean to *lust,* as well as *to covet*, as is further
expounded upon below.

On stating that "to lust after" – or *covet* – a
woman as being akin to adultery of the heart, Christ
was referring to those who *covet* an already married
woman (MATTHEW 5:28) – especially when God hates

---

having *nothing* whatsoever to do with sexually fantasizing about
a person, pornography, having premarital sex, or anything else of
the sort – but rather with cheating on your own wife or going after
your neighbor's spouse instead – either in thought or in action. We
must *always* pay attention to context [see also note 34 on page 71]
– lest we wind up assuming things that are *not there*, and repress
ourselves and everyone else in the process – and thus condemn
the innocent for the sake of our own form of religiosity, legalism,
taboo, and what we have become comfortably used to assuming –
while neglecting what God might *really* be saying to us.

divorce in that He is in the business of building relationships and not tearing them down. This point is further strengthened by the fact that the translation of Christ's Aramaic speech used the Greek word *epithumeo*, which is translated as "to covet", "to set one's heart upon", or to "strongly desire" something – *epithumeo* having commonly been used *interchangeably* with both "to covet" and "to lust after". Furthermore, the word was frequently utilized in both negative as well as positive contexts – to where the idea of *intent* to pursue (or follow through) with *action* being strongly present in its use – in other words, doing whatever is required to *achieve* or manifest the intent or desire.

As such, the word "lust" here would seem to mean that one "desire with intent at following through with", and not merely to "form a mental image" – as is commonly (but most likely erroneously) assumed. Therefore, it can be seen that one having erotic thoughts does *not* mean that one is committing any wrongdoing – it is not what Christ likely meant at all. Furthermore, Christ used this very *same* word in other occasions – in a positive sense – where he was not talking about anything remotely to do with sex in any way whatsoever. Such occasions included the time when he stated, during the Last Supper, that "I have earnestly desired [*epithumeo*] to eat this Passover with you before I suffer...";[15] and

---

[15] LUKE 22:15

on another occasion he stated that "... many prophets and righteous men desired [*epithumeo*] to see what you see, and did not see it...".[16] Thus *epithumeo* was again used interchangeably by Christ in referring to both good and bad forms of "strong desire" – which again is *also* used in the Greek language to mean "covet" – as we see on Paul's likewise using *epithumeo* in reference against coveting a neighbor's property in ROMANS 7:7 and 13:9 – the act of *coveting* (to desire an object *specifically* belonging to, possessed by, or already owned by another) to the ultimate ends of wishing to have *someone else's* possession as one's own being against one of the Ten Commandments not to covet another's personal belongings as found in DEUTERONOMY 5:21, which states that "YOU SHALL NOT COVET YOUR NEIGHBOR'S WIFE, AND YOU SHALL NOT DESIRE YOUR NEIGHBOR'S HOUSE... FIELD... SERVANT... OX... DONKEY... OR ANYTHING THAT BELONGS TO YOUR NEIGHBOR."

Now, taking the fact that Christ stated that we are not to "lust after" – or alternatively *covet* – a woman lest we commit adultery – adultery again being defined as sex with another who is *already* married – in the famous Sermon on the Mount,[17] and that if we are angry with our brother without cause, that we are essentially committing murder[18]

---

[16] MATTHEW 13:17

[17] As having been correctly translated into the Greek-interpreted word *epithumeo* from his Aramaic-spoken sermon.

[18] Again, the sixth Commandment stating that we must not commit murder, as put in DEUTERONOMY 5:17 – as he continued in his teaching on these Commandments given to the world from days of old.

in our hearts[19] – it would therefore seem that the
Sermon on the Mount which mentions the above (as
well as other) issues was in fact a *commentary* or
teaching that focused on the Ten Commandments, and
on the ultimate *two* commandment which sums the
aforementioned up in one sentence: this being, to love
the Lord your God with all your heart, and to love your
neighbor as yourself.[20]

Taking all of these factors into consideration, it
can be implied that what Christ referred to in regards
to "lusting" – or rather *coveting* – after a woman
as committing *adultery* with her in one's heart was
in reference to the commandment not to "covet your
neighbor's wife" – to where one must not covet, or
"lust after", the *wife* of another in wishing to take
her as one's own – much as one must not be angry without cause against the innocent,[21] lest one
commit murder in one's heart (again, against the
commandment not to murder). Thus Christ seems
to be stating that the Ten Commandments apply
even in one's deliberate *intention* to break them –
such as the seventh commandment stating that one
must not commit adultery (again, having an affair
with one who is already married, or even conversely
separating from one's lawful wife in divorce without

---

[19] See MATTHEW 5:21-22.
[20] MATTHEW 22:34-40
[21] As in MATTHEW 5:22.

just cause) – to where such "coveting" of another person's spouse without express permission is akin to breaking *both* the commandments against coveting as well as adultery in one's heart. In this respect, it is presumptuous and out of context to simply *assume* that Christ was stating we must not look, appreciate, or maybe even think sexual thoughts regarding a woman (or man) who is *not* already married – and whom we do not wish to "steal" from anyone else who they are presently with, nor break up a relationship by cheating with him or her apart from their partner's knowledge or consent. In other words, to love our neighbor as ourselves extends to not having affairs with someone who already belongs to someone else, to where we would likewise not want anyone to cheat with our own spouses without our consent in like manner – which of course does not involve pornography, premarital sex, and the like.

Therefore, many feel that Christ was specifically referring to the coveting for *possession* of another's legal wife – which has nothing to do with thinking sexual thoughts about women (or men) in general in and of itself – and all to do with the initial mental desire to *take* possession the spouse of another by deliberately *intending* to have an affair with him or her... which can (and likely will) of course *eventually* lead to adultery in whatever way one defines it as. It is the deliberate *intent* at coveting another's spouse towards the end result of having an affair of some type that makes one commit adultery in one's heart – much as it is the deliberate *intent* at truly *hating* another person without cause which causes one to commit murder in one's heart – both of which break the ultimate command to love one's neighbor as oneself.

Thus putting the concept of both "coveting after" and "adultery" together in contextual summation to said Sermon on the Mount, let us now take a wider-view look from the context of it all. As Christ goes on to explain in his next major topic during the Sermon on the Mount – to divorce one's wife is like-wise akin to committing adultery.[22]   He says this without even *mentioning* sex as having anything to do with committing adultery in and of itself when considering other times in which he speaks on divorce, as previously explained – though the cause of being sexually unfaithful *without permission*[23] is in fact a legitimate reason to divorce, as he states.   Thus it would seem that even adultery is not being referred to *solely* in the context of having sex with one who is already married – as "committing adultery" would commonly be thought of today – but rather with the

---

[22] See MATTHEW 5:31-32.

[23] This distinction being made here as the Judeo-Christian Bible never outlaws polygamy. As such, would a "swingers" couple be committing adultery by sharing their spouses with others if done without duress and in full agreement by mutual consent? I don't know. God alone must be your guide on such matters.

act of *separating* from one's spouse without just cause
– whether or not sex with another has anything to
do with it. Nevertheless, having sex with one who
is *already* married, or if oneself is married, would
likely constitute adultery – at the very least if done
without the free-will and non-manipulated consent
and awareness of the other spouse in question.

Therefore, on taking the *definition* of adultery into
more thoughtful consideration – that is, "the voluntary sexual intercourse between a *married* person and
someone *other than* his or her lawful spouse",[24] as
well as the definition of *epithumeo* as interchangeably
meaning "to covet'" – it would seem reasonable to
conclude that adultery – and "lusting after" – herein
has *nothing to do* with either premarital sex (again,
whether gay, lesbian, or straight) *nor* with sexual
thought and fantasy *whatsoever* – especially as Christ
never seemed to have ever made an issue out of
premarital sex between two unmarried consenting
adults in the first place[25] – but rather to do with the
intent to *take* another's *already* lawful wife as one's
own either through an affair (again, whether or not
sex is involved) or by deliberately desiring to cause a
break-up in an already established relationship.

---

[24] Webster (as in n. 1 on page 152).

[25] See also the excellent book Thelos, *Divine Sex: Liberating Sex from Religious Tradition* (as in n. 8 on page 158).

In conclusion, anything desired is lust – it can be good or bad – depending on the object of that desire (in this case, if the "object" of your affection is *already* in a legally binding, closed relationship). We lust for food, water, stability, happiness, love...and sex. These things in and of themselves are not wrong to pursue as normal parts of life and of being human. Yet if the object of our desire is a married man or woman, and we actively seek to "have" or "possess" him or her in a relationship of our own, and set our hearts to that end, than it probably constitutes what Christ was talking about in regards to "lusting after a woman". But to think erotic thoughts about a person in general is not what Christ was talking about at all if we consider all relevant angles.

In conclusion, "lusting after", within the considered context of what Christ was speaking about – namely the Ten Commandments – is equal to coveting what *belongs to* another. Christ is addressing the act of *coveting*, not sexual fantasy in and of itself – *nor* of premarital sex between two unmarried people (again, whether gay or straight) for that matter. For sexual fantasies are thoughts that do not have intentions to *possess* or *go after* another's wife in and of themselves. In contrast, the intent at *attaining* another's wife (or if married, another woman at the detriment of breaking one's own marriage vows – and thus divorcing),[26] is the form of lust, or coveting, that was being spoken of. Again, nothing to do with pornography, sexual fantasy, premarital sex, admiring the sexual beauty of another, or anything of the sort – and all to do with the *active* pursuit and intent of breaking a marriage vow – hence the *specific* use of the word "adultery" in combination with *epithumeo* (to covet another's possession). Sexual fantasy in and of itself has nothing to do with it – pure and simple.

A.5 You did *What*? How?

It should also be mentioned – for the sake of those who may be wondering – and most people do – that *neither* the Judeo-Christian Bible, *nor* Christ himself, *ever* list masturbation, oral sex, or anal sex (nor any other form of sexual act) as being forbidden at all[27] – they *never* condemn anyone for these natural joys, and they do *not* call any of these as sin in any way whatsoever... despite what you might have been misled to think from certain "religious" circles. Furthermore, God gave us a mind to use, to where common sense will tell us that, as natural and God-given methodologies of self-expression and creativity

---

[26] When as previously stated: God is in the business of building relationships – between Him and ourselves, as well as between each other – and not on tearing them down.

[27] See Milgrom (as in n. 14 on page 41).

in life, none of these are sinful or wrong in the grand
scheme of reality – but are rather genuine alterna-
tives to committing *true* wrongs on earth towards our
fellow man... such as committing violence, bullying
one's co-worker, condemning the innocent; as well as
inflicting oneself with heart disease and the likelihood
of strokes, cancers, and all forms of health problems
stemming from both a sexually-repressed lifestyle
and the resultant mental instabilities from caring too
much about what others do in the privacy of their
own bedrooms. Why do some *always* have to forcibly
fuse the physical with the spiritual. For even Christ
distinguished both when declaring that all foods are
clean (so that we are not bound by the Holiness Code
decree not to eat pork and the like any longer), and
that it is what comes *out* of the heart of someone
[as he clarified in verses 17-23] that truly defiles the
individual, when he stated:

> ... LISTEN TO ME, ALL OF YOU, AND UNDERSTAND:
> THERE IS NOTHING OUTSIDE THE MAN WHICH CAN
> DEFILE HIM IF IT GOES INTO HIM; BUT THE THINGS
> WHICH PROCEED OUT OF THE MAN ARE WHAT
> DEFILE THE MAN. IF ANYONE HAS EARS TO HEAR,
> LET HIM HEAR.[28]

Thus if any of the aforementioned sexual vehicles
towards human interaction and the expression of

---

[28] MARK 7:14-16

both love and desire were sinful at all, surely the scriptures would have *clearly* stated so in no uncertain terms. They *never* do. In fact, they seem to actually *encourage* sexual experimentation, as we will see. Anyone who states otherwise is playing religion and placing the traditions of man above God-given common sense, as well as putting a burden on man which is impossible to bear,[29] as Christ himself put it in regards to man-made doctrine. Such a person would do well to take a *sincere* second look at scripture before their stress levels continue to rise and their arteries begin to clog. They are no good dead to anyone – and would be more useful alive and doing *genuinely* good works that *actually matter* for the Kingdom of God – such as loving their neighbor, taking care of the sick and dying, visiting the prisoner, and educating the world about how Christianity is *not* a faith of sexual-repression, but rather of liberation, truth, fundamental reality, internal peace, happiness, and confidence.

Therefore, the Bible clearly does *not* prohibit specific sexual acts (such as oral or anal sex, the use of over-priced sex toys, spindles of joy, positions in bed, exotic locations, and so forth) between consenting individuals – as many non-Christian religions often do ad nauseam in this day and age, while ignoring (or worse... having the gall to condemn) the nature and

---

[29] See note 1 on page xii.

psychology of God's own creation.[30] Anyone stating otherwise is *again* playing religion and placing the traditions of man (herein how religion in general has traditionally looked at such topics while revealing just how sexually repressed some truly are) before common sense, what is natural, and what God has created – to where God's power and sexual design is flat-out ignored and trumped by religious legalisms that cannot even be backed up by scripture whatsoever – such man-made taboos being nothing more than the inventions of puritanical religious leaders who understand very little of what the Bible actually has to say about one of God's most liberating and life-affirming gifts to us all.[31]

On the *other* hand, as stated, the Judeo-Christian Bible seems to actually *encourage* sexual play and experimentation. Three very *brief* examples of this

---

[30] See also Thelos, *Divine Sex: Liberating Sex from Religious Tradition* (as in n. 8 on page 158).

[31] See also Countryman (as in n. 12 on page 28); which clearly shows through the examination of scripture that *none* of these things are ever forbidden in the Judeo-Christian Bible, how *all* positions and methods are natural and God-given, and how our modern sexual hangups have been caused *not* by scripture, but by mankind's own invented legalisms – such religious legalities which completely go against God's purpose and design for us on having a healthy, *non*-religious, but faith-based personal relationship with Him – such religious-borne hangups, doubts, and needless guilt that condemn, stifle, and repress the innocents amongst us all who are only being the human beings that they were created to be. It is also worth looking at the excellent book Thelos, *Divine Sex: Liberating Sex from Religious Tradition* (as in n. 8 on page 158) – which affirms the same.

include oral sex as mentioned in Songs of Solomon 2:3, which states – in regards to oral sex being performed on a male:

> As an apple tree among the trees of the wood, so is my beloved among young men. With great delight I sat in his shadow, and his fruit was sweet to my taste.[32]

as well as Songs of Solomon 4:16, in regards to oral sex being performed on a female:

> ...Blow upon my garden that its fragrance may be wafted abroad. Let my beloved come to his garden, and eat its choicest fruits.[33]

and Songs of Solomon 8:2, which states, within the context of a romantic rendezvous:

> ...I would give you spiced wine to drink, the juice of my pomegranates.[34]

But if you would like to look further into just how sexually-liberating the Judeo-Christian Bible truly is in regards to all things sex, take a look at the excellently-researched, comprehensive, and detailed books on these and many other related joys as *Divine Sex: Liberating Sex from Religious Tradition,*[35] as

---

[32] Songs of Solomon 2:3

[33] Songs of Solomon 4:16

[34] Songs of Solomon 8:2

[35] Thelos, *Divine Sex: Liberating Sex from Religious Tradition* (as in n. 8 on page 158).

well as *Dirt, Greed, and Sex: Sexual Ethics in the
New Testament and Their Implications for Today*[36] –
both of which further explain in great and clear detail
how *none* of these things are *ever* forbidden in the
Judeo-Christian scriptures, how *all* sexual positions
and methods are natural and God-given, and how
our modern sexual hangups have originated *not* from
scripture, but from mankind's own invented legalisms
and traditions[37] which have nothing whatever to do
with either the Jewish or Christian grass-roots origins
of faith.

Sexually-restrictive taboos and self-righteously "puritanical" traditions of man that did not even *exist*
in the Christian faith until centuries *after* Christ[38]
not only condemn and repress the innocents amongst
us who are both faithful to God and realistically
accepting of His gift of life – a gift that is *meant* to be
lived and not wasted – they likewise smear the name
of Christianity, totally misrepresent its very foundations, and are the modern-day stumbling blocks

---

[36] Countryman (as in n. 12 on page 28).

[37] See also Raymond J. (as in n. 35 on page 73); which
explains in great detail how such legalistic traditions of man
first infiltrated the church in the fourth century AD via the
Roman Greco Platonic philosophy – which had absolutely *nothing*
whatsoever to do with either Christ *or* the Bible. For even the
early Christians who existed *before* such an external influence
towards the religion appeared held to liberal views on sex that
today would make many *modern-day* Christians either blush or
self-combust (in more ways than one) in their church pews.

[38] See Ibid.; as well as note 35 on page 73.

to both homosexuals *and* heterosexuals... many of whom have a totally *skewed* view about both God and faith in this day and age precisely because of such groundless restrictions. Sometimes one might think one is still living during the Dark Ages. And ironically, *true* Christianity does not even have anything to do with it in the first place!

So have fun if you so wish, be safe, respect your sexual partners (and make sure they *always* respect *you*), and be creative – as God intended it to be – whether you are gay *or* straight. Apologies for bringing up such explicit topics of reality – but the innocent have been condemned for far too long – and continuously stumble with needless guilt and fear by the dishonest intents of the many religiously-imposing traditionalists amongst us who have never bothered to intelligently and contextually study their own scriptures in the first place. Don't be one of them. Life's much too short as it is.

A.6   Tolerance and Forgiveness

All this being said, one thing must be remembered, especially in regards to those who have in fact committed adultery by having an affair without one's spouse's knowledge or consent. Christ stated, in regards to life in general:

BE MERCIFUL, JUST AS YOUR FATHER IS MER-
CIFUL. AND DO NOT JUDGE, AND YOU WILL NOT BE
JUDGED; AND DO NOT CONDEMN, AND YOU WILL
NOT BE CONDEMNED; PARDON [literally meaning
release], AND YOU WILL BE PARDONED. LUKE 6:36-
38

I know – easier said then done for many who have
found out that their spouse has had a long-running affair without one's knowledge. Yes, Christ stated such
circumstances *are* a legitimate reason for divorce. But
if there is *still* any ounce of love between you two
– might it not be worthwhile trying again? Maybe
going to a marriage counselor? Maybe taking a break
for a while to think things through? Maybe talking
about it, as well as looking into how you *still* might
or might not feel about each other – before deciding to
separate? Maybe laying down mutually agreed-upon
ground rules for communication?

Though he *did* provide a legitimate way out, would
God not prefer forgiveness and having both of you
move on together as a team where such things might
possibly actually *bring* you closer together as a couple
as well as strengthen who you are as individuals –
if that is possible? Maybe not – only you and God
know, depending on what is going on in your life.
Certainly not if you're being physically abused, that's
for sure! If that were the case, as stated, Christ
again provides a way out in divorce as – in cases

of physical abuse and bullying – one has essentially *already* been abandoned by one's spouse by his or her abuse in action – but one is never abandoned by God... though it might sometimes feel like it. But assuming such abuse is not the case – is it worth it for the children... so long as honesty becomes your mutually agreed-upon standard? Could talking about the little things that build up over time to where unspoken issues "unexpectedly" explode be the cause of it all? Could giving each other more private space be the answer? Whatever the answer, if you are in such a situation in regards to contemplating divorce for whatever reason, I pray that God be with you at this time, and that He *guide* you to make the right decisions – *whatever* they might be – that He allows you to *see* what He might *want* you to see – and that He gives you *His* peace which "transcends all understanding"[39]... in Jesus name.

As for those who have as yet not caught on or understood that you are free to have premarital sex so long as you do not commit adultery (by having it with one who is already in a marriage), I would ask that you re-read this Appendix, and stop going through the needless guilt of being the human God intended for you to be. So long as you are "loving your neighbor as yourself" and thus respect both yourself as well as the other person (whomever that might be), and he or she

---

[39] PHILIPPIANS 4:7

respects *you* as well – to where you do not get involved
with a game-player, manipulator, abuser, or otherwise
dangerous individual (remember, there are a lot of
wolves out there... but many good people as well) –
and so long as you love yourself enough to take both
sexual as well as mental and emotional precautions
– take care, be balanced, don't be *overly*-excessive to
the point of addiction, and *be yourself*. To those who
would judge these same good people who are simply
living life, I would remind you of Christ's words as he
said:

> ...BUT IF YOU HAD KNOWN WHAT THIS MEANS,
> 'I DESIRE MERCY, NOT SACRIFICE', YOU WOULD
> NOT HAVE CONDEMNED THE INNOCENT. MATTHEW
> 12:6-7

Yet who *is* innocent in this world? If Christ looks at
the heart – with all of its fallacies and shortcomings –
and straight into the soul of good intent *despite* many
imperfections, and yet *still* declares one as "innocent"
– than should we not do the same?

> BE MERCIFUL, JUST AS YOUR FATHER IS MERCI-
> FUL.[40]

Again, be tolerant towards others' views on sex (for
to be tolerant or merciful *even* to the intolerant is
what is meant to love your neighbor as yourself)

---

[40] LUKE 6:36

– but don't let others make you stumble in your relationship with God because of their own hand-ups and self-imposed restrictions due to their lack of understanding, assumptions, traditions, and taboos. And don't let the "religious" turn you into a sexually-repressed human being when God made and intended that we use His gift of sex as a normal and essential part of life – especially when neither Christ himself, nor the Judeo-Christian Bible, ever restricted any form of sexual activity except adultery, sex for pay, [41] incest, bestiality, rape, and sex involving the worship of idols.

A.7   Christ's Message was About Love, *not* Sexual Abstinence

Christ, through his words and actions, showed the world that he was *not* a sexual "prude" of religious and preachy obsession (as most of the "religious" are today), that he understood and accepted man's God-given desires, and that he was much more con-cerned about *genuine* sins that separate us from a

---

[41] Though Christ was a true and *genuine* friend and confidant to prostitutes who *never* condemned nor judged them – for to God such as these are *much more* valuable as individuals whom He unconditionally loves, and who He longs to care for *despite* popular social "opinions" regarding their chosen way of making a living, that He would rather they trust in His care and friendship instead of being maligned by an oftentimes cold and unmerciful world.

relationship with God and from each other while
making clear that, as stated beforehand, God is in
the business of building relationships, and not tearing
them down.   Christ's focus on sins mostly involved
such things as arrogant pride, idolatry, the love for
money to where the poor take a back-seat to one's
dedication to riches, greed, jealousy, all manifestations of social injustice, the neglect of the sick and
desperate-hearted in our midst, religious-borne self-
righteousness, violence, and all falsely-pious forms of
religious hypocrisy.   As such, revisit your views on
sex not from religion's perspective, but rather from
Christ's own words and actions.   Just don't go after
someone else's wife, nor go behind the back of your
own spouse when this has not been agreed-upon in
your relationship.

And most importantly, don't let them make you
stumble in your relationship to God because of your
sexual lifestyle. This cannot be emphasized enough,
as many are constantly being turned off to God on
a daily basis because of the many man-made and in-
validated traditions and hang-ups, taboos, put-downs,
religious lies and self-righteous anti-sex obsessions
of mankind from virtually all organized religions ...
and God has nothing to do with *any* of it – as Christ
himself made clear. You don't have to be like *them*
– the self-appointed "religious" – to love God and to
have a personal relationship with Him. You don't have

to have a sexless life in order to talk to Him as your Heavenly Father who cares for and loves you above all else. You can even talk to him *during* sex if you wish! He is *always* with you, no matter where you are or what you are doing.

In fact, He does *not* want you to be like them at all, but rather to be *yourself* as He has made you...just as you are.   For He Himself loves you unconditionally...just as you are, and just as you are *meant* to be.   That is the message of Christ, and that alone.   That is the message for *all* faiths. That is the message of genuine and *unconditional* love and acceptance – without preconditions or strings attached. All you have to do is put your trust in Him. What have you got to lose?

CEASE STRIVING, AND KNOW THAT I AM GOD.
PSALM 46:10

Appendix B

Cults, Control Freaks, and the Moderate

It is better to walk alone with God, I believe, if the *only* other alternative you face is to be amongst a group of worshipers who are stuck in playing games of *organized religion* and mind control, instead of focusing on Christ and his unconditional love – and who dominate, judge, condemn, and attempt with all their might to change you and who you are – particularly when they load unnecessary mental burdens, doubts, and false guilt on your mind and spirit – to where the spiritual satisfaction and joy you once had gets into danger of becoming dulled and lukewarm, to eventually get ripped away from you altogether by the very people who claim to be doing "God's work". It is not worth wasting your time arguing with these people about matters of doctrine when they themselves have become dead to Christ and the simple faith that he taught. For their focus is on *religion* instead of on God. Their goal is submission instead of acting on love. They have exalted themselves above God Himself, as they hang on to misquoted scripture in order to keep their pride and worthless "reputations" at the expense of the poor in spirit.

It is these kinds of people who seek to "win over souls" at any cost, to *then* simply draw them away from their new-found relationship with God as they make His very children stumble with unnecessary confusion, guilt, self-doubt, and fear brought on by the firm grasp of man's traditions and meaningless, repetitive rituals.[1] They have forgotten who they are meant to represent. For Christ is *not* a God of fear – but of love, peace, and mental and spiritual tranquility and balance.[2] And they make the world stumble as a consequence of their pious, self-righteous, and religiously-judgmental words.

---

[1] As Christ stated:

> And when you are praying, do not use meaningless repetition as the Gentiles do, for they suppose that they will be heard for their many words. So do not be like them; for your Father knows what you need before you ask Him. MATTHEW 6:7-8

[2] Jesus said:

> ...I came that they may have life, and have it abundantly. JOHN 10:10

B.1   When Religion Does More Harm than Good

Do you hear phrases such as "theocracy", "submit", "obey", "under authority", "robbing God", "Five-Fold ministry", and "apostolic mandate" in the church you go to? You may be involved with the "Super Apostles" and "neo-Pentecostal" movements. The man-made, non-biblical concept of "Super Apostles" is a model of heretical fanaticism that is currently spreading throughout the globe by certain *so-called* "Christian" church groups who are likewise known for separating families, making sincere believers in Christ stumble in their faith, and destroying individual lives. It is very much encouraged that the reader, especially the Christian-based reader, take a look at the eye-opening and revealing site CULTWATCH.COM,[3] which speaks in detail about the damage these and other groups have caused Christians world-wide. In fact, the site sums this up excellently in the following quote:

> The spiritual dynamics of Mind Control result in the Christian having the Holy Spirit replaced in their life by the counterfeit of an earthly middleman. The Super Apostle and his leaders insert themselves between the Christian and God. Instead of the Christian being convicted by the Holy Spirit the Christian receives false conviction from men. Christians are told by men what they have done wrong

---

[3] *Cult Watch*. ⟨URL: http://www.cultwatch.com⟩

according to the rules those men have invented. This leads to a spiritual dependency on those men rather than a dependency on the Holy Spirit. Christians, who should become strong, instead become weaker as their dependency on their leaders and the church organization grows. Of course this is what the leaders desire since it makes these Christians more controllable. However this spiritual counterfeit is a slow poison that crushes the spirit of the Christian. After the "Honeymoon" period with the church is over, the Christian emerges to find they are struggling to meet the standards of the group. They are told that life should be perfect, but it is not. The constant meetings, the controlling pressure, the stress, and the condemnation from the leadership, takes its toll. The Christian tries harder. But fails again and again. Finally the Christian burns out. Too long they have been running on man-made power rather than God's. "If this is Christianity", they say, "then I don't want to have anything to do with it!" So they reject Jesus and turn to the world. Convinced that the counterfeit they experienced was Christianity they never again consider following our Lord. Not all reject Christianity, but those who return to biblical churches struggle to cope. They suffer depression and feelings of guilt. The preaching of their false apostle is still in their head. Those who have wasted years in the counterfeit group feel a tremendous sense of loss. They take much time to recover. This is the fruit of Mind Control, numerous shipwrecked Christians.[4]

---

[4] *CultWatch.com: Attack of the Super Apostles!* ⟨URL: http://www.cultwatch.com/superapostles.html⟩;   this   quote

I could not have described it better myself! And this is usually the outcome from being involved in any cult from whatever relevant church, political movement, corporation, or marketing strategy it may take the form of. The likes of these are but wolves in sheep's clothing. Generally speaking, any church, group, or organization that attempts to *separate* families on its own accord; that shuns the *entirety* of television, music, or the arts as a whole; and that feels its group is the *only* sect that is following God – and that all others are going to burn, are heretical, or deceived – should *probably* be avoided. I know I would...why should I suffer unnecessarily...and why should you?

B.2   A Cult's Red Flags

Furthermore, tell-tale signs that a church – or even a political movement, "self-help" or "counseling" organization, or corporate environment or scheme – may in fact be a form of cult include the following:

- *deception*: It uses deception in order to hide the truth of what it is really about, or what it truly represents, so that others are initially *willing* to join.

---

first used by permission in author's previous work as granted from the originator and copyright holder CULTWATCH.COM.

- *exclusivity*: To where non-members are seen as 'in the wrong' – or on their way to hell-fire – if they are not part of or agree with that particular church.[5]

---

[5] Even *some* who believe in evolution seem to sometimes do this, as they oftentimes consider creationists as either idiots or religious freaks while at times treating evolution as a religion in its own right. Yet many prominent scientists now conclude that it is statistically *much more* probable that the over six million individual parts of a disassembled Boeing 747 aircraft strewn throughout a junk yard would *by sheer chance* be put back together again to perfectly re-build the original aircraft through a passing tornado – than for evolution to have taken place without an intelligent designer being involved... whatever our earth's age may be. See the highly analytical works of Fred Hoyle, *Mathematics of Evolution*. Acorn Enterprises Llc., 1999; Lee M. Spetner, *Not by Chance*. Judaica Press, 1997; Michael J. Behe, *Darwin's Black Box: The Biochemical Challenge to Evolution*. 2nd edition. Free Press, 2006; and Idem, *The Edge of Evolution: The Search for the Limits of Darwinism*. Free Press, 2007.

If you are interested in this subject, I would encourage you to look into the references cited above, as many scientists bent on proving evolution have as a result come to a personal belief in a Creator due to the widespread factual inaccuracies of the theory that, though proven untrue in recent decades, are still being taught in our schools and universities as fact. Many now feel that it would take much more *faith* in believing we came from apes than to accept God's involvement in our creation. Consequently, the theory of evolution has *unnecessarily* had a major negative affect on our present global societies and governments – even Hitler used the theory to argue that the Nazis were part of a superior race, as he hoped to induce the "continued" evolutionary development of a perfect and superior Aryan race on earth. Consequently, due to the widespread belief that there is no Creator, and that we are here purely by chance without anyone to account to – it's every man for himself, survival-of-the-fittest takes precedence over social responsibility, and both money and power over "the weaker" have now *for some* become the prime motivators of societal progression and individual aspirations above personal accountability.

- *using fear, intimidation, and personal character assassination:*
  Through attacking one's motives, character, and sincerity.

- *"love bombing":* Displaying an instant and seemingly "intimate" friendship with someone they have just met; while attempting to control the private lives and relationships of its members in regards to existing family and friends.

- *controlling information:* Such as restricting what one can and cannot read, watch, and research; while claiming that only *their* literature (their own books, magazines, tapes, DVD's, and so forth) hold the truth.

- *lack of confidentiality:* To where members are *instructed* to report on confidential conversations between themselves and target recruits to a designated leader.

- *controlling member's time:* By *constantly* involving them in meetings, lectures, conferences, classes, and so forth – while limiting the time that a member is able to spend with his or her own family, personal friends, leisure activities, and work responsibilities.

- *pressure selling:* Through *overly-enthusiastic* meetings and *intensive* – at times to the point of even being aggressively "in-your-face" – one-on-one conversations where one is asked to reveal one's personal life, thoughts, and intentions; or where one is coercively made to feel inferior, weak, or guilty if one does not agree, show mutual enthusiasm... and eventually obey whatever non-sense they are demanding of their members.

- *contribution-pressure:* Using guilt, fear, and other manipulative techniques to acquire your money.[6]

As Christ himself said:

> THEY [the religious leaders] TIE UP HEAVY BURDENS AND LAY THEM ON MEN'S SHOULDERS, BUT THEY THEMSELVES ARE UNWILLING TO MOVE THEM WITH SO MUCH AS A FINGER. BUT THEY DO ALL THEIR DEEDS TO BE NOTICED BY MEN.[7]

and,

> BUT WOE TO YOU, SCRIBES AND PHARISEES, HYPOCRITES, BECAUSE YOU SHUT OFF THE KINGDOM OF HEAVEN FROM PEOPLE; FOR YOU DO NOT ENTER IN YOURSELVES, NOR DO YOU ALLOW THOSE WHO ARE ENTERING TO GO IN.[8]

God never intended that we should live separate from the rest of the world, but that we should be a light in the darkness, and this without being subjected to all the enchainments that come with organized religion. God intended that we have a personal and intimate relationship with *Him*... without being "religious" in any way. Religion is for those that need to be led, and for such as these, that can

---

[6] The above points are summations from the site *How Cults Work*. ⟨URL: http://howcultswork.com⟩. It is greatly encouraged that the reader look through it in detail. As its author rightly states: "Remember, people are not perfect, but if they employ them constantly you are most likely dealing with a cult."

[7] MATTHEW 23:4-5

[8] MATTHEW 23:13

oftentimes become a dangerous thing to depend on indeed. For when dependence on religion takes the place of a dependence on God and His guidance; when dependence on hard text and legalistic approaches to doctrinal interpretation takes the place of being led by the Spirit of Truth (or Holy Spirit) that was promised to all who would receive Him; all bets are off... *anything* can happen. And it usually does. Be *in* the world, but not *of* the world. This does *not* mean believers should isolate themselves in religion. And as Jesus also stated in JOHN 17:15 when he was praying,

> I DO NOT ASK YOU TO TAKE THEM OUT OF THE WORLD, BUT THAT YOU PROTECT THEM FROM THE EVIL ONE.

B.3   *Some* Churches are Alright

Yet it must be emphasized that not every church or religious organization is like the few bad apples that fit such tell-tail signs – in fact, most are not. There are *many* fine, sincere, and genuinely loving and balanced churches out there that are *not* radical or manipulative; and that – from the Christian perspective – teach Christ's love, mercy, and grace as *he* taught it.

Examples of church denominations that are at times considered to be well-balanced, sincere, non-manipulative, sensible, and in addition *genuinely* welcoming of homosexual people would be segments of the Church of England (or *Anglican/Episcopalian* Church) – such as those found specifically in both Great Britain and the U.S. – as well as *some* branched Pentecostal,[9] Quaker,[10] and *few* Catholic churches – to name several.[11]   Even amongst your own chosen denomination – for those that might have one – you may sometimes find a local church that is hospitable and accepting of homosexual people and who know their Bible well – but *please* always take caution until you know for sure when visiting a local branch.

Furthermore, the Metropolitan Community Church (MCC)[12] is truly a God-send church for LGBT[13] people that *especially* emphasizes acceptance of *all* regardless of sexual orientation – MCC churches almost always having a sensible approach to faith, biblical perspectives on both Christ and the Bible, a balanced approach to genuine love, and being welcoming of

---

[9] In particular, the Affirming Pentecostal Church, the Global Alliance of Affirming Apostolic Pentecostals (GAAAP), and the Fellowship of Reconciling Pentecostals International (RPI) – but *not* The United Pentecostal Church International. So be careful not to get them confused!

[10] Also known as *Society of Friends* – especially many of those in the UK, Canada, New Zealand and Australia – but *not* always in the U.S. or Africa.

[11] For a comprehensive list, including a helpful color-coded graph, see Wikipedia, *List of Christian denominational positions on homosexuality*. Wikipedia, 2011 ⟨URL: http://en.wikipedia.org/wiki/List_of_Christian_ denominational_positions_on_homosexuality⟩.

[12] *Metropolitan Community Church*. ⟨URL: http://www. mcchurch.org⟩.

[13] Lesbian, Gay, Bisexual, and Transgendered

all regardless of ethnicity, race, sexual orientation, and creed throughout the world. Nevertheless, as with any denomination (as all things in life), there is no guarantee that a *particular* local congregation or group from the aforementioned denominations is in fact rational, understanding, respectful, or genuine – so that you must always use your common sense and good judgment.

Therefore, it is obviously imperative that you always use that rational brain and intuition that God has given you. And if you *do* choose to visit or join a church, it is suggested that you do so through prayer, shrewd observation, a balanced degree of common sense without initially being either too open nor too suspicious, cool rationality, patience, and an independent mind. And above all else, always keep in mind that nobody is perfect.

So if you *do* find a group that encourages and acknowledges you as a *genuine* child of God without judging your personal life and intentions – when you know that you have in fact come to Him in sincerity and truth – than more power to you! You don't *need* religion to have a personal one-on-one relationship with Christ, as was meant to be – but fellowship is always important and beneficial when done with the *right* people. So long as this remains *consistent*, and they do not come between you and how God is leading your life on a *personal* level – than stick with them unless God tells you otherwise.

B.4   But One does not *Need* Religion to Speak to God

We don't *need* a self-serving, politically-correct preacher telling us how God leads us or how He wants us to live our lives for His glory – and this out of love for Him, and not by deceptive obligation to some institution or the traditions of mankind. We *already* know that! For it is Christ's promised Spirit of Truth (or Holy Spirit) that personally and directly reveals *all things* to us – as Christ clearly explained.[14]   If you have sincerely opened your door to God with the *simplest* of faith – simply by putting your trust in Him and saying "Father, I'm yours, come into my life", He *has* now become part of your life, and *will* guide you into *all* truth if you just stop and listen to His voice within. Talk to Him as you would a loving friend, and He *will* reveal Himself to you, and will show you the abundant purpose He has for your life... guaranteed! All you have to do is ask.

Don't let them take your faith away, nor prevent you from *continuing* to speak to your Father – who loves, understands, and cares for you so much more

---

[14] See note 23 on page 33.

than anyone else on earth *ever* will... no matter *who* you are, what battles you've fought, or where you presently find yourself in life's journey.

So if the sort of *religious* group you find yourself in consists only of those who have long forgotten about coming to God as a child, and who have replaced Him with the worship of church bureaucracy, attempted control of members' personal lives, memorized verses to judge and implement fear to those who do not obey, and religious-borne piety and self-righteousness – than get out of their, and don't look back – and know that God is *with you*, and that if it is *His* will for you to find a place that worships Him in spirit and in truth, than He *will* lead you to it. And *if* it is God's will that you take some months – or even years — off from any involvement with organized religion, than He will make this clear to you as well. As is stated:

> TRUST IN THE LORD WITH ALL YOUR HEART, AND
> LEAN NOT ON YOUR OWN UNDERSTANDINGS. IN
> ALL YOUR WAYS ACKNOWLEDGE HIM, AND HE WILL
> DIRECT YOUR PATH.[15]

You don't *need* organized religion. No one does... no one *ever* did. Christ *himself* made this clear. You are flesh and spirit – so worship Him *not* in temples built by man, but *"in* spirit and in truth",[16] as he so clearly said. Not to say you should not associate with

---

[15] PROVERBS 3:6
[16] See note 3 on page 5.

others who are worshiping Him in this way as well
and who treat you as a responsible and intelligent
human being who is led by God as He sees fit. They
are out there. And again, fellowship – with the *right*
people – *is* of utmost importance for encouragement,
support, and friendship. But if you presently find
yourself in the "wrong" *religious* crowd – who's god *is*
religion – detach from them before they do you and
your family – and especially your mind and soul – any
more damage. Detach from those, the religious and
fanatical that would hinder your mind and soul – and
find people who respect *you*, *your* choices. . . and most
of all, your Heavenly Father.

Appendix C

Some Interesting Facts

To those who may be interested, this appendix section provides some interesting analysis of facts involving scripture, messiahship, world history, and how the story of mankind fits into it all. Furthermore, its subject matter is a mere taster for the vast amounts of resources that are readily available for the world to see – a very small number of which are referenced herein as starting places for your own research – these resources being both fascinating in detail and scope, as well as solidly reputable as analytical examinations relating to said topics.

It is felt that this section, rather than being a diversion from the main topics of this book, complement the issues discussed herein due to much of this work's reliance on both scripture as well as Christ himself. Furthermore, this section can also be seen as an addendum to Chapter 1 in that it provides some interesting analysis as to topics that are often *misused* in causing one to fall away from personal faith due to the misinformation presented by groups and denominations attempting to essentially "brainwash" a target into membership in their respective sect. In like manner, it is also a complementary section to appendix B in providing the reader with a brief analytical viewpoint of the person of Jesus Christ from both a mathematical, as well as historical perspective – rather than from what a theologian may "claim" as fact. And so we begin.

C.1   What *are* the Odds?

The appearance of Christ amongst mankind was spoken of centuries – even millennia – before his arrival by many detailed and specific prophecies that stated such things as found in ISAIAH 9:6-7, which says:

> TO US A CHILD IS BORN, TO US A SON IS GIVEN, AND THE GOVERNMENT WILL BE ON HIS SHOULDERS.   AND HE WILL BE CALLED WONDERFUL COUNSELOR, MIGHTY GOD,[1] EVERLASTING FATHER, PRINCE OF PEACE. OF THE INCREASE OF HIS GOVERNMENT AND PEACE THERE WILL BE NO END. HE WILL REIGN ON DAVID'S THRONE AND OVER HIS KINGDOM, ESTABLISHING AND UPHOLDING IT WITH JUSTICE AND RIGHTEOUSNESS FROM THAT

---

[1] See also sub-section C.3 on page 214; this Appendix.

TIME ON AND FOREVER. THE ZEAL OF THE LORD
ALMIGHTY WILL ACCOMPLISH THIS.

Of the hundreds of *specific* prophecies about Jesus
Christ that were all fulfilled by this *one* particular
individual when considering planet earth's *entire* civilized history – prominent mathematicians and statis-
ticians have stated that the mathematical probability
that even a *single* human being in the entirety of
the populated history of our planet to be able to
legitimately fulfill even a mere *eight* of the over three-
hundred of these *distinct* prophecies (astoundingly,
Christ single-handedly fulfilled *each* and every one of
them) is so purely *astronomical* in statistical number – this being one chance in one-hundred-million-
billion, or 10^{17} ... or to put it bluntly –

one in 100,000,000,000,000,000

– that the odds of this occurring are millions of times
greater even if one takes into account the cumulative
population of *all* of mankind who has ever existed in
earth's history as well as who are likely to *ever* exist
into the future of humankind. In other words, from
a purely mathematical perspective, this essentially
excludes anyone else that has ever (or *will ever*) live
on earth but Jesus of Nazareth *alone* as being able to
fulfill said prophecies as the promised Jewish Messiah
who was specifically written about by many different
authors during a vast span of time numbering many

centuries before his birth. As is explained herein, no other person in history can make such a claim, let alone be prophesied about in such specific and non-ambiguous detail hundreds – and in some cases even *thousands* – of years before appearing on the planet...no one. It is essentially a mathematical *impossibility*.

One of many such mathematicians, the distinguished Dr. Peter Stoner,[2] who had twelve graduate classes consisting of six-hundred students work out such a calculation over several years based solely on a mere *eight* prophecies alone (out of over three-hundred) concerning Christ, and who submitted these same calculations and results to the American Scientific Affiliation for independent verification – who in turn verified and finally concluded after careful and lengthy examination that these calculations and results were indeed accurate and dependable – explained just how large a number 10^{17} is, as he states:

> Let us try to visualize this chance. If you mark one of ten tickets, and place all of the tickets in a hat, and thoroughly stir them, and then ask a blindfolded man to draw one, his chance of getting the right ticket is one in ten.

---

[2] Chairman of the Departments of Mathematics and Astronomy at Pasadena City College until 1953; Chairman of the science division, Westmont College, 1953-57; Professor Emeritus of Science, Westmont College; and Professor Emeritus of Mathematics and Astronomy, Pasadena City College.

> Suppose that we take 10^{17} silver dollars and
> lay them on the face of Texas. They will cover
> all of the state two feet deep. Now mark one
> of these silver dollars and stir the whole mass
> thoroughly, all over the state. Blindfold a man
> and tell him that he can travel as far as he
> wishes, but he must pick up one silver dollar
> and say that this is the right one. What chance
> would he have of getting the right one? Just the
> same chance that the prophets would have had
> of writing these eight prophecies and having
> them all come true in any one man, from their
> day to the present time, providing they wrote
> using their own wisdom.[3]

Surely everyone would take on any financial investment with these odds when the possibility of *failure*
is only one in 10^{17}. And this is the kind of sure
investment that God offers us in putting our trust in
Christ, his Son.

Stoner's (and his students') initial calculations
were based on a mere *eight* Messianic Old Testament
prophecies as a *conservative* examination and study
– which again worked out to a result of one in 10^{17}.
He then performed a similar calculation based on
forty-eight of said prophecies and came up with the
result of 10^{157}. Anything over 10^{50} is considered a

---

[3] Peter Stoner, *Science Speaks: Scientific Proof of the Accuracy of Prophecy and the Bible*. Moody Press, 1969; pp. 106-7. See also this same book for free on-line at Idem, *Science Speaks: Online Edition*. November 2005 ⟨URL: http://www.geocities.com/ stonerdon/science_speaks.html⟩.

mathematical *impossibility*, and yet Christ fulfilled *all* of the over three-hundred very distinct prophecies in the Old Testament that describe in great detail the characteristics, origin, birth, life, death, works, and social contexts of the coming Messiah – just as fingerprint and DNA evidence combined to find a fit in a court case is a sure enough thing to come to a definitive conclusion concerning one's identity well *beyond* reasonable doubt – in fact, enough so to send someone to his death in a murder case in a nation that might adopt the death penalty.

Of the hundreds of said prophetic verses that would support these findings, the following are but a *few*, such as ISAIAH 9:6 (as previously quoted), which states that one *particular* human being in earth's history would be born who would be *both* fully God and fully man... or God incarnate. Who else in history could such a claim apply to but Christ alone – especially on considering the fact that only he ever fulfilled *each and every one* of the Messianic prophecies in earth's entire history? Yes...

> FOR A CHILD WILL BE BORN TO US. A SON WILL BE GIVEN TO US... AND HIS NAME WILL BE CALLED... MIGHTY GOD, ETERNAL FATHER, PRINCE OF PEACE...

MICAH 5:2 states that he would specifically be born in *no other place* but Bethlehem alone, and that he in fact existed *"from days of old"*... in other words, from the beginning of time:

> BUT AS FOR YOU, BETHLEHEM EPHRATHAH, TOO
> LITTLE TO BE AMONG THE CLANS OF JUDAH, FROM
> YOU ONE WILL GO FORTH FOR ME TO BE RULER IN
> ISRAEL. HIS APPEARANCES ARE FROM LONG AGO,
> FROM DAYS OF OLD.

ISAIAH 7:14 states that he would be born of a virgin, and that *again*, he would be called God *Himself*, as per the significance of the name *Immanuel* – meaning "God with us":

> THEREFORE THE LORD HIMSELF WILL GIVE YOU
> A SIGN: BEHOLD, A VIRGIN WILL BE WITH CHILD
> AND BEAR A SON, AND SHE WILL CALL HIS NAME
> IMMANUEL.

ISAIAH 53:3-7 describes the purpose and details of his crucifixion:

> HE WAS DESPISED AND REJECTED BY MEN, A MAN
> OF SORROWS, AND FAMILIAR WITH SUFFERING.
> LIKE ONE FROM WHOM MEN HIDE THEIR FACES
> HE WAS DESPISED, AND WE ESTEEMED HIM NOT.
> SURELY HE TOOK UP OUR INFIRMITIES AND CAR-
> RIED OUR SORROWS, YET WE CONSIDERED HIM
> STRICKEN BY GOD, SMITTEN BY HIM, AND AF-
> FLICTED. BUT HE WAS PIERCED FOR OUR TRANS-
> GRESSIONS, HE WAS CRUSHED FOR OUR INIQUI-
> TIES; THE PUNISHMENT THAT BROUGHT US PEACE
> WAS UPON HIM, AND BY HIS WOUNDS WE ARE
> HEALED... HE WAS OPPRESSED AND AFFLICTED...
> YET HE DID NOT OPEN HIS MOUTH; HE WAS LED

LIKE A LAMB TO THE SLAUGHTER. AND AS A SHEEP
BEFORE HER SHEARERS IS SILENT, SO HE DID NOT
OPEN HIS MOUTH. [4]

In addition, other ancient scriptures spanning multiple Old Testament books, authors, and wide-ranging
time-spans numbering hundreds – even *thousands* –
of years, prophecy about the coming Messiah in more
specific details such as:

- ISAIAH 7:14, which proclaims how he would be
  born of a virgin;

- GENESIS 12:1-3 & 22:18, specifying how he would
  be a descendant of Abraham;

- of the tribe of Judah, as stated in GENESIS 49:10;

- and of the house of David (as we have seen in
  Chapter 6) in II SAMUEL 7:12-16;

- and that he would be taken to Egypt as a child
  as in HOSEA 11:1;

- how Herod would kill male infants under two
  years old, hoping to kill the promised Messiah
  who had just been born, as in JEREMIAH 31:15;

- how he would be heralded by God's messenger
  (John the Baptist), as in both ISAIAH 40:3-5 as
  well as in MALACHI 3:1;

---

[4] Frank Charles D.D. Ph.D. Thompson, editor, *Thompson
Chain-Reference Bible: New International Version.* Zondervan
Bible Publishers, 1983.

- how he would perform miracles such as making the blind physically see again, healing the deaf, making the lame and paralyzed walk once more; unbridling the tongue of the mute, and so on as per ISAIAH 35:5-6;

- that he would preach the good news (ISAIAH 61:1),

- as well as minister in Galilee (ISAIAH 9:1),

- and cleanse the temple from all of its robbery, self-righteousness, and religious fervor that had lost its child-like faith as in MALACHI 3:1;

- as well as ZECHARIAH 9:9, which explains how the promised Messiah would enter Jerusalem as a King riding on a donkey;

- while ZECHARIAH 13:7 details how everyone – including his own apostles – would soon abandon him to be crucified,

- as he was being rejected by his own people of faith – the Jewish nation – as per PSALM 118:22;

- ZECHARIAH 11:12, which states he would be betrayed for *exactly* thirty pieces of silver;

- that this betrayal would come from a close friend, as in PSALM 41:9;

- ZECHARIAH 11:13, detailing how this price would then be given to buy a Potter's field after the Jews rejected the betrayer's (this having turned out to have been Judas) return of said money; and how this blood-money would be cast back onto the floor of the temple;

- how he would furthermore be rejected (ISAIAH 53:3) and become silent before those who falsely accused him (ISAIAH 53:7), and would consequently be mocked (PSALM 22: 7-8), beaten (ISAIAH 52:14), and spit upon (ISAIAH 50:6);

- and how he would be crucified with thieves – yet he would pray for his persecutors as per ISAIAH 53:12;

- PSALM 22:18, which details how his clothing would be divided up amongst his persecutors, and that they would cast lots for the possession of torn fragments of said clothing while he was still on the cross;

- PSALM 22:16, which details how both his hands and feet would be pierced during his crucifixion;

- PSALM 69:21, foretelling in detail how gall and vinegar would be given to him to drink while he hung on the cross;

- PSALM 34:20, stating how none of his bones would be broken through this entire ordeal;

- ZECHARIAH 12:10, explaining that his side would be pierced while he was still barely alive;

- ISAIAH 53:9, regarding his being placed in a rich man's tomb after his eventual death; and

- ISAIAH 26:19, PSALM 16:10, HOSEA 6:2, PSALM 68:18, and PSALM 110:1 – foretelling his glorious resurrection after three days; of which both the New Testament as well as secular writers affirm this having taken place as having been witnessed by over five-hundred witnesses – many of whom were later systematically persecuted and brutally killed for what they claimed to have seen with their very own eyes. I wouldn't be so willing to lay my life down for something I *knew* not to be true, would you?

...and so the list goes on – through to the rest of the three-hundred-odd specific and detailed prophecies spanning centuries and authors living historically apart from one another – all of which pointing to one single man in a future time in history who would fulfill each and every one of them without question or ambiguity. These, the prophecies that, in all mathematical probability, can never – nor *will* ever – be attributed to anyone else but Jesus Christ of

Nazareth alone. Jesus, the uniquely unrivaled One who, from two millennia ago, has influenced mankind more than anyone else in the entirety of human history *ever* has... to this very day. What *are* the odds?

C.2   The Authenticity of a Man

Similarly, Dr. Will Durant, one of the most highly-regarded and probably *the* most widely-read historian in the last century himself stated, regarding the *authenticity* of the life of Christ, and the *eye-witness* testimonies recorded by those who were there, and who were likewise willing even to die for a cause they *knew* to be true – as most of them eventually did... for who in their right mind would be willing to die for a cause they *know* is a lie...

> In the enthusiasm of its discoveries, the higher criticism has applied to the New Testament texts tests of authenticity so severe that by them a hundred ancient worthies, Hammurabi, David, Socrates, would fade into legend... no one reading these scenes can doubt the reality of the figure behind them ... that a few simple men should in one generation have invented so powerful and appealing a personality, so lofty an ethic and so inspiring a vision of human brotherhood, would be a miracle far more incredible than any recorded in the Gospels. After two centuries of higher criticism, the outlines of the life, character and teachings of

Christ remain reasonably clear and constitute the most fascinating feature in the history of Western man.[5]

With these odds *overwhelmingly* in favor of Him, I believe that Christ deserves *at least* a cursory listening to, and that he most likely *knows* what he is talking about in regards to life, love, health, homosexuality as being a characteristic from birth, sex, happiness, what makes for world peace – and everything that we are, have ever been, and have the potential to *become* as distinct individuals. I would certainly rather consider what he *himself* said, and how he lived, rather than hearing some self-righteous or narrow-minded preacher on a pulpit of organized religion, that's for sure[6] – though not all preachers are like this, and many are in fact kind-hearted, non-judgmental, and *genuine* followers of God. Again, by their fruits you *will* know them. Even so, one must, as previously stated, use one's common sense and good judgment. For you cannot always depend on someone just because they call themselves a "Christian", or just because they wear ornate robes and know how to sing like an angel.

---

[5] Will Durant, *Caesar and Christ - A History of Roman Civilization and of Christianity from their Beginnings to A.D. 323 (Story of Civilization)*. Simon & Schuster, 1944.

[6] See also Lee Strobel, *The Case for Christ*. Zondervan, 1998; as well as the excellent video documentary under the same title.

But on Christ you *can* always depend upon. He is the same yesterday, today, and forever. He *never* changes. The God of the universe who stooped down to such lowly highs to carry those like you and I – and all of this because of His undying love for each and every one of us... and love alone.

C.3   God *and* Man?

But as many cults have become stumbling blocks to the faith of many[7] who seek respite from an unpredictable world, to where they are often more than happy to kick a seeker of truth precisely when she or he is already down – especially in regards to questions revolving around the Deity of Christ – the following outline hierarchy is reprinted from Cyrus I. Scofield, *Scofield Reference Bible*. Oxford University Press, 1917, now in public domain:

The Deity of Jesus Christ is declared in Scripture:

(I) The Old Testament both intimates and explicitly predicts His Deity.

(a) The theophanies intimate the appearance of God in human form, and His ministry in this form to man (GENESIS 16:7-14; 18:2-23, especially verse 17; compare 32:28 with HOSEA 12:3-5; EXODUS 3:2-14).

---

[7] See Appendix B.

(b) The Messiah is expressly declared to be the Son of God (PSALM 2:2-9), and God (compare PSALM 45:6-7 with HEBREWS 1 :8-9; PSALM 110:1 with MATTHEW 22:44; ACTS 2:34 and HEBREWS 1:13; PSALM 110:4 with HEBREWS 5:6; 6:20; 7:17-21; ZECHARIAH 6:13).

(c) His virgin birth was foretold as the means through which God could be Immanuel, God with us (compare ISAIAH 7:13-14 with MATTHEW 1:22-23).

(d) The Messiah is expressly invested with the divine names (ISAIAH 9:6-7).

(e) In a prophecy of His death He is called the "man, My Associate" (compare ZECHARIAH 13:7 with MATTHEW 26:31); and

(f) His eternal Being is declared (compare MICAH 5:2 with MATTHEW 2:6; JOHN 7:42).

(II) Christ Himself affirmed His Deity.

(a) He applied to Himself the Jehovistic "I AM" (JOHN 4:26; 6:20; 8:24,28,58; 18:5,6). The pronoun "He" appears in translation (4:26 and 18:5,6), but not in the Greek. In 8:56-59 the Jews correctly understood this as the Lord's claim to full Deity (compare JOHN 10:33).

(b) He claimed to be the *Adonai* of the Old Testament (MATTHEW 22:42-45. See GENESIS 15:2, note).

(c) He asserted His identity with the Father (MATTHEW 28:19; MARK 14:62; JOHN 10:30). That the Jews so understood is shown by JOHN 10:31-33; 14:8-9; 17:5.

(d) He exercised the chief prerogative of God – the forgiveness of sins (MARK 2:5-7; LUKE 7:48-50).

(e) He asserted omnipresence (MATTHEW 18:20; JOHN 3:13); omniscience (JOHN 11:11-14,

when Jesus was fifty miles away; MARK 11:6-8);
omnipotence (MATTHEW 28:18; LUKE 7:14; JOHN
5:21-23; 6:19); mastery over nature, and creative
power (LUKE 9:16-17; JOHN 2:9; 10:28); and

(f) He received and approved human worship of Himself (MATTHEW 14:33; 28:9; JOHN
20:28-29).

(III) The New Testament writers ascribe divine
titles to Christ (JOHN 1:1; 20:28; ACTS 20:28; RO-
MANS 1:4; 9:5; II THESSALONIANS 1:12; I TIMOTHY
3:16; TITUS 2:13; HEBREWS 1:8; I JOHN 5:20).

(IV) The New Testament writers ascribe divine
perfections and attributes to Christ (MATTHEW
11:28; 18:20; 28:20; JOHN 1:2; 2:23-25; 3:13; 5:17;
21:17; HEBREWS 1:3, 11-12 with HEBREWS 13:8;
REVELATION 1:8,17-18; 11:17; 22:13).

(V) The New Testament writers ascribe divine
works to Christ (JOHN 1:3,10; COLOSSIANS 1:16-
17; HEBREWS 1:3).

(VI) The New Testament writers teach that
supreme worship should be paid to Christ
(ACTS 7:59-60; I CORINTHIANS 1:2; II CORINTHI-
ANS 13:14; PHILIPPIANS 2:9-11; HEBREWS 1:6; REV-
ELATION 1:5-6; 5:12-13).

(VII) The holiness and resurrection of Christ
confirm His Deity (JOHN 8:46; ROMANS 1:4).

After all, as JOHN 1:1-2 & 10-12 & 14 puts it all so very
well:

IN THE BEGINNING WAS THE WORD, AND THE
WORD WAS WITH GOD, AND THE WORD WAS GOD.
HE WAS WITH GOD IN THE BEGINNING. . . HE WAS IN
THE WORLD, AND THOUGH THE WORLD WAS MADE

THROUGH HIM, THE WORLD DID NOT RECOGNIZE
HIM. . . YET TO ALL WHO RECEIVED HIM, TO THOSE
WHO BELIEVED IN HIS NAME, HE GAVE THE RIGHT
TO BECOME CHILDREN OF GOD. THE WORD BE-
CAME FLESH AND LIVED FOR A WHILE AMONG US.
WE HAVE SEEN HIS GLORY, THE GLORY OF THE ONE
AND ONLY SON, WHO CAME FROM THE FATHER,
FULL OF GRACE AND TRUTH.[8]

Therefore, neither let the world, nor religion, nor principalities and powers that may be, nor the homophobes in our midst, nor society, nor the media, nor your boss and work environment, nor radicals, nor terrors, nor crimes and persecutions, nor self-doubt or low self-confidence, nor riches, nor poverty, nor cults, nor denominations or books or manuals, nor divisive argument, nor peace, nor war – hinder your faith in your First Love ... the best and most loyal friend you will *ever* know. Yes, He who formed you and *knew* you – *intimately* – before you were even born, and who loves you oh so *very* much – always and forever – *just* as you are.

C.4   But how Reliable *is* the Modern Bible?

The reliability of the modern Bible *cannot* be disputed. We *have* the original documents in tangible

---

[8] JOHN 1:1-2, 10-12, and 14.

– *physical* – form strewn throughout the world in climate-controlled vaults, secure archives, museums, national library safes, banks, and other locations that shall remain nameless. It is a modern-day common argument to state that the Bible has been translated so many times that it cannot be relied upon any longer. It is understandable when a lay person has doubts if they have not looked into this matter; but it is an altogether clear-cut and outright deception fueled by non-investigative ignorance and unfounded assumptions when such a claim is made by those in the media when they clearly cannot be bothered to check their facts before broadcasting such nonsense. Literally *thousands* of original manuscripts exist in tangible and superior condition throughout the world dating back all the way to Genesis, and – *despite* the explanations herein regarding the mistranslations of few modern versions to do with certain words such as "homosexuality", "sodomy", or "fornication" – which are sporadic issues at best where the overall context and meaning has never been lost or put into dispute – the modern-day Bible reads pretty much as it did from when the various books that compose it were first written.[9]

Did you know that the modern-day Judeo-Christian Bible can be trusted and relied upon as reflecting

---

[9] See also F.F. Bruce, *The Canon of Scripture*. IVP Academic, 1988.

the *original* manuscripts much more so than any classic literature *including* Homer, Aristotle, Pliny, and Tacitus? For instance, the world has at its disposal more than 14,000 *original* Old Testament manuscripts dating back several millennia. Furthermore, over 5,300 original manuscripts of the New Testament exist today that go back all the way to the first century – yes, we actually *have* the original compositions as well as painstakingly-replicated word-for-word, hand-written copies that match up to said originals *precisely*. Even secular historians going back *before* the second century AD make direct references to and quote biblical text – and furthermore speak of Christ in great and meticulous detail.[10] These include Josephus the famous Jewish historian, Tacitus, Suetonius, and Pliny Secundus, who was a Roman governor; as well as Irenaeus, Julius Africanus, Tertullian, and Clement of Rome.

Furthermore, archaeological evidence that support biblical stories, peoples, and history abound to such an extent that even archaeologists such as Sir William Ramsay who have previously set out to disprove biblical claims have as a result of their extensive research become believers in both biblical accuracy as well as in the very faith that is contained within its pages.

---

[10] See also Bruce Metzger, *The Text of the New Testament: Its Transmission, Corruption, and Restoration*. 4th edition. Oxford University Press, 2005.

For even many a skeptic has become a believer on realizing that specific biblical predictions dating all the way back to the Old Testament have so far come true; including prophecies concerning Israel, Babylon, the Phoenician city of Tyre, Sidon... as well as prophecies about governments, kingdoms, and individuals such as Christ himself to statistical probabilities that affirm the impossibility for the fulfillment of said prophecies to have occurred by sheer accident.[11]

All original, as well as later, biblical manuscripts agree in 99.5% of the text – which is a great accomplishment on the part of scribes and scholars throughout the ages who had meticulous techniques to both copy as well as check and re-check for errors. From the .5%, most arguable discrepancies involve either word order or spelling – or word meaning as is the case with original language used involving the topics mentioned within this work – but even this is *minuscule* on considering just how robust history has been able to keep later copies of the Judeo-Christian Bible so true to original manuscripts – especially as many other secular ancient manuscripts cannot often make such a claim – not to 99.5% accuracy at least. Furthermore, any said discrepancies or questions of meaning are usually now contained in footnotes in

---

[11] See also Bruce M. Metzger, *The Canon of the New Testament: Its Origin, Development, and Significance.* Oxford University Press, April 1997.

most of today's Bibles – such as seen in those notes re-quoted from versions within this work, for example.[12]

Hence, the reliability of the Bible cannot be dis-puted. Mankind is not so ignorant as to be incapable of doing a competent job at passing down both original physical manuscripts through thousands of years, as well as accurately copying the same verbatim into other languages. Furthermore, the originals we have include the Old Testament Hebrew and New Testament Greek manuscripts, to where any dispute regarding language translation is *easily* able to be compared and put to rest with the same – as it always is on producing third-language translations throughout the world. What many should probably be disputing is *not* the faithfulness of the current Bible to original scrolls, but rather the faithfulness of modern-day doctrinal claims from many newly-found "religions" to common sense ... or at the very least, whether or not honey is *indeed* fattening.

C.5   Who *can* You Trust?

Some say all written scripture is God's authority, and they tell the truth when even Christ quoted the Old

---

[12] See also the short, comprehensive, exceptional, and easy to digest Frederick Fyvie Bruce, *The New Testament Documents: Are They Reliable?* Wilder Publications, 2009; as well as Bart D. Ehrman, *The New Testament and Other Early Christian Writings*. Oxford University Press, 1998.

Testament, and in addition to this clearly stated that
we must listen to *him*, because *he* has the words of
life,[13] and he himself *brings* about life, and *is* life.[14]
Even the Father is said to have stated of Christ, "This
is My beloved Son, in whom I am well pleased. Listen
to *Him*".[15] Of course, He did *not* say "listen to Paul", or
to your church leader, or to popular theological opinion
in the place of Christ. No. He said, "Listen to *Him*".

Thus neither Christ, nor the Father, nor anyone
else in the Bible, ever mention letters written by
anybody coming *after* Christ as their words being
considered the exclusive and unadulterated words
of God – though God *does* inspire mankind, as He
does even today. For even Paul himself stated that
"all scripture is inspired by God"[16] when he clearly
referred to the Old Testament scriptures; as he was
not so arrogant as to consider his *own* letters to the

---

[13] As Jesus said,

> It is the spirit that gives life; the flesh is useless. The
> words that I have spoken to you are spirit and life.

[14] As Jesus said, right before he raised Lazarus from the dead
– one of many accounts where he did the same on other occasions:

> I am the resurrection and the life. Those who believe
> in me, even though they die, will live; and everyone
> who lives and believes in me will never die. Do you
> believe this? JOHN 11:25-26

[15] MATTHEW 3:17; MATTHEW 17:5; LUKE 3:22; MARK 9:7.
[16] II TIMOTHY 3:16

early churches to be the unadulterated words of God
– though they too were inspired.

For it is Christ who *is* the Word of God. Christ is
the *Living* Word of God,[17] and none other. We must
be careful not to substitute this for something else.[18]
To do so, I believe, is to commit idolatry... placing
man's words and traditions above God's, as the Jewish
leaders commonly did in Christ's days – and as many
preachers, self-proclaimed "gurus", religious speak-
ers, denominations, and religions still do today. For
only Christ can make such a claim – considering what
we have seen in this Appendix as his having been
the undisputed Messiah that was talked about in the
Old Testament, knowing of the works he performed,
and realizing the Deity that was inherent within him
exclusively and without rival... God in man, in the
literal sense.

That is why we must take care what we listen
to – be it current opinion regarding homosexuality;
be it your preacher, teacher, or church leaders; be it
popular opinion or the latest religious craze... or be it
this very book even. For on Christ we have the Word of
God – to those who are believers – and by the guidance
of his Spirit of Truth are we set free from the con-

---

[17] As quoted in sub-section C.3 on page 214 from JOHN 1:1-14.
[18] See also note 3 on page 126.

fusions of contradictory theology, assorted religions, innumerable philosophies, and volatile opinions.[19]

Why else would he have told us not to call anyone on earth our teachers,[20] as those who have opened their hearts to him already *have* a teacher and leader – the living Christ himself – who can *never* be substituted for either religion or the fallacies of man. To do so is to risk turning what Christianity is meant to stand for from its very *origin* as the good news of God drawing mankind to Himself through a simple child-like faith – and into an *organized* and oftentimes imperfect form of religion that is based on man's traditions and dogmas – most likely Paulinian in style, as opposed to Christ-like in spirit and purpose. For Christ did not come to burden man's souls with yet *another* organized form of religion... but to *free* them *himself*, as he *alone* does the work in our lives.[21]

---

[19] As Jesus clearly stated,

> Therefore, everyone who hears these words of Mine and acts on them, may be compared to a wise man who built his house on the rock. And the rain fell, and the floods came, and the winds blew and slammed against that house; and *yet* it did not fall, for it had been founded on the rock. Everyone who hears these words of Mine and does not act on them, will be like a foolish man who built his house on the sand. The rain fell, and the floods came, and the winds blew and slammed against that house; and it fell – and great was its fall. MATTHEW 6:24-27

[20] As seen in note 23 on page 33.

[21] For as Christ himself explained,

And herein lies the critical and most obvious difference between any *religion*'s irrational and very much *burdensome* demands regarding the subjugation to a set of behaviors and rules within an organized list of recommendations, long-held traditions, and man-made inventions – as opposed to Christ's teaching of a simple, *child-like* faith and completely surrendered *reliance* on our Creator; as well as a self-acceptance that does not oppress the ego – but rather expands and matures it into what God meant for mankind to be *from the beginning* – free, and without man-made enchainments nor fragile dependencies to rigid and uncompromising systems and traditions.

In essence, let Christ *himself* be your authority. For he *is* the Living Word of God – the Holy Spirit being *his* Spirit within each and every one who opens their door to him *just as they are* and at *whatever point* in life they find themselves at – whether good or bad, happy or sad, victorious or tragic, isolated or within a crowd, intelligent or plain, religious or not. It is *his* Spirit of Truth who reminds us of everything that he taught the world in the Gospels. And it is *his* Holy Spirit who leads us all – without *any* exclusion

---

Come to me, all you that are weary and are carrying heavy burdens, and I will give you *rest*. Take my yoke upon you, and *learn* from me; for I am gentle and humble in heart, and you will find rest for your souls. For my yoke is *easy,* and my burden is *light.*
MATTHEW 11:28-30

or exception whatsoever – into *all* truth in a day
and age where empty hearts and minds abound, and
where multiple voices will often tear down those who
would quickly put too much trust in their words and
philosophies. . . yet they never *can* overcome. For he
himself has said,

> THESE THINGS I HAVE SPOKEN TO YOU, SO THAT
> IN ME YOU MAY HAVE PEACE. IN THE WORLD YOU
> HAVE TRIBULATION, BUT TAKE COURAGE, I HAVE
> OVERCOME THE WORLD.[22]

Yes sir, as has aptly been said before, "Let God be true
and every man a liar."[23]

I believe that it is *not* Paul – nor his words,
opinions, and occasional admonishments – nor anyone
else who has ever – or *will* ever – live, who is truth.
For it is only Christ – God incarnate who stooped
down so low in order to *unconditionally* love a weary
soul such as I – who has plainly said,

> I AM THE WAY, AND THE TRUTH, AND THE LIFE.
> NO ONE COMES TO THE FATHER EXCEPT THROUGH
> ME.[24]

---

[22] JOHN 16:33

[23] As expressed by Paul himself in ROMANS 3:3-4,

> What then? If some did not believe, their unbelief
> will not nullify the faithfulness of God, will it? May
> it never be! Rather, let God be found true, though
> every man be found a liar. . . . .

[24] JOHN 14:6

Hence, I believe that those who *genuinely* come to God in spirit and in truth – whatever religion they might claim to subscribe to – come to and *through* Christ, because Christ and the Father *are* one. And anyone who honors the Son and what He stands for honors the Father who sent him. Only you and God know if you have ever done so yourself... maybe you don't even *realize* that you have, I don't know. No one can judge you. For only *He* sees your heart, and nobody else. But such lasting assurance, peace, and rock-solid stability from *within* cannot be had by anything else, nor through any "religion" that this world has to offer – as when one comes to the Son directly and says, "Jesus, thank you for your unconditional love for me. I don't have anything to offer back to you. But I welcome you into my life. I am yours."

It becomes a *personal* experience – an *intimate* one-on-one... without *any* sign or notion of religion, without the approvals of mankind, and without doctrine and theology. But those who have *somehow* – in simplicity of spirit and sincerity of truth – turned to the Father and honor the Son – in whatever unique way that God reaches out to each and every one of us – I believe are part of the family of Christ... no matter who they are or what they might claim to "believe", know, or subscribe to from the viewpoint of society, religion, or mankind. For those who do *not* honor the Son obviously do *not* honor what he stands for, and

therefore cannot in their hearts honor the Father who
sent him. For, as Jesus plainly said,

> I AND THE FATHER ARE ONE. [25]

Furthermore, Christ told us:

> FOR JUST AS THE FATHER RAISES THE DEAD AND
> GIVES THEM LIFE, EVEN SO THE SON ALSO GIVES
> LIFE TO WHOM HE WISHES. FOR NOT EVEN THE
> FATHER JUDGES ANYONE, BUT HE HAS GIVEN ALL
> JUDGMENT TO THE SON, SO THAT ALL WILL HONOR
> THE SON EVEN AS THEY HONOR THE FATHER. HE
> WHO DOES NOT HONOR THE SON DOES NOT HONOR
> THE FATHER WHO SENT HIM. TRULY, TRULY, I SAY
> TO YOU, HE WHO HEARS MY WORD, AND BELIEVES
> HIM WHO SENT ME, HAS ETERNAL LIFE, AND DOES
> NOT COME INTO JUDGMENT, BUT HAS PASSED OUT
> OF DEATH INTO LIFE. [26]

And as he put plainly:

> BLESSED [happy] IS HE WHO DOES NOT TAKE OF-
> FENSE AT ME.[27]

Again, it is a *personal* experience. Without religion.
Without ceremony. Without preconditions. Jesus
Christ *is* the *only* way to the Father because he *is*
the Father. Paul is not the way, and neither is any
self-proclaimed cult or religious "guru", nor religious
teacher, nor preacher, nor biblical commentaries, or
whatever form of organized religion there may be.

---

[25] JOHN 10:30; or literally translated to "one essence", or
"unity".

[26] JOHN 5:21-24

[27] MATTHEW 11:6

It is the difference between a true follower of Christ and what he stands for, as opposed to merely calling oneself a "Christian".   Personally, I would rather simply be called a *follower* of Christ. For than, even if I stumble and fall, the religious cannot judge nor condemn me, because my relationship is not with them, but with *Him*.   And thus, if and when I *do* faulter, still I see him there with outstretched arms saying "wipe your tears away, and do not fear. See, I *never* left you, and never will. I love you."

Anyhow, that is what *I* believe as based on both the Gospels and the words of Christ, and *especially* based on *my* personal experience. Right... it *is* such a personal experience that only you and God can truly know. God sees straight *past* one's religious beliefs, dogmas, traditions, fears, doubts, errors, wrongs, and intentions... and straight *into* the heart. How is *your* heart with God? If you are not sure, go ahead and simply *ask* Him to show Himself to you, and He *will* reveal Himself to you... guaranteed. For,

> ...ANYONE WHO COMES TO ME I WILL NEVER DRIVE AWAY.[28]

Christ warned us that there would be *many* false prophets, false teachers, and false religions who would appear and mislead *many* – even the elect[29] – these

---

[28] JOHN 6:37
[29] See MATTHEW 24:23-27.

many diverse (and oft-times *divisive*) voices whom billions would look to for answers while taking their focus away from the Spirit of God before Christ comes back to earth – and that we must be careful and discerning, and not run after them; but that we must *personally* keep our focus on Him alone without either being fearful or confused by what we see and hear in the world today. But as few lines in a pertinent song state:

> Rest in your faith, My peace will come to you
>
> I know there are so many things that you've been hearing
>
> But you just hold on to what I told you.[30]

Put your trust in Christ, and Christ *apart from* organized religion and all the time-wasting nonsense that comes with it – and you will *never* go wrong...

> *whatever* your sexuality
>
> *whatever* your religious background
>
> *whatever* your doubts
>
> *whatever* you have done
>
> *whomever* you are.

...all else is pulp fiction and the philosophies of man.

---

[30] Keith Green, *When I Hear the Praises Start: For Him Who Has Ears to Hear Album*. Sparrow Records, 1977.

All in all, look to the one who is the same yesterday, today, and forever – and leave the rest to wallow in their own self-imposed constraints.

> PEACE I LEAVE WITH YOU; MY PEACE I GIVE TO YOU. I DO NOT GIVE TO YOU AS THE WORLD GIVES. DO NOT LET YOUR HEARTS BE TROUBLED, AND DO NOT LET THEM BE AFRAID.[31]

---

[31] The words of Jesus Christ to all who may come without exception; as per JOHN 14:27

Part II

Resources

THIS IS THE VERDICT: LIGHT HAS COME INTO THE WORLD, BUT MEN LOVED DARKNESS INSTEAD OF LIGHT BECAUSE THEIR DEEDS WERE EVIL. EVERYONE WHO DOES EVIL HATES THE LIGHT, AND WILL NOT COME INTO THE LIGHT FOR FEAR THAT HIS DEEDS WILL BE EXPOSED. BUT WHOEVER LIVES BY THE TRUTH COMES INTO THE LIGHT, SO THAT IT MAY BE SEEN PLAINLY THAT WHAT HE HAS DONE HAS BEEN DONE THROUGH GOD.

Jesus Christ, JOHN 3:19-21

Bibliography

Cult Watch. ⟨URL: http://www.cultwatch.com⟩.

CultWatch.com: Attack of the Super Apostles! ⟨URL: http://www.cultwatch.com/superapostles.html⟩.

Ex- Jehovah Witnesses Community of Survivors. ⟨URL: http://www.exjws.net⟩.

Freeminds.org: Watchers of the Watchtower World. ⟨URL: http://www.freeminds.org/doctrine/jesus.htm⟩.

How Cults Work. ⟨URL: http://howcultswork.com⟩.

Metropolitan Community Church. ⟨URL: http://www.mccchurch.org⟩.

Recovery from the International Churches of Christ: rightcyberup.org. ⟨URL: http://www.rightcyberup.org/⟩.

Reveal. ⟨URL: http://www.reveal.org⟩.

The Thesaurus Linguae Graecae. ⟨URL: http://
www.tlg.uci.edu/⟩.

Triumphing Over London Cults: Education and
Counselling on Cults & ICC. ⟨URL: http:
//www.tolc.org/⟩.

Whosoever: An Online Magazine for Gay, Lesbian,
Bisexual, and Transgender Christians. ⟨URL:
http://www.whosoever.org⟩.

Would Jesus Discriminate. ⟨URL: http://www.
wouldjesusdiscriminate.com⟩.

Aarons, Leroy, Prayers for Bobby: A Mother's
Coming to Terms with the Suicide of Her Gay
Son. HarperOne, 1996.

Alexander, Marilyn B., We Were Baptized Too:
Claiming God's Grace for Lesbians and Gays.
John Knox Press, 1996.

Alexandria, Clement Of, Paedagogus III [The
Instructor]. Kessinger Publishing, 2004.

Alexandria, Clement of, The Stromata III.
Kessinger Publishing, 2004.

Armstrong Percy III, William, Pederasty and
Pedagogy in Archaic Greece. University of
Illinois Press, 1998.

Attridge, Harold W. et al., editors, The Harper-
Collins Study Bible, Revised Edition: New
Revised Standard Version. Harper Collins
Publishers, 2006.

Behe, Michael J., Darwin's Black Box: The Biochemical Challenge to Evolution. 2nd edition.
Free Press, 2006.

Behe, Michael J., The Edge of Evolution: The Search for the Limits of Darwinism. Free Press, 2007.

Berenbaum, Michael, A Mosaic of Victims: Non-Jews Persecuted and Murdered by the Nazis. I.B. Tauris, December 1990.

Boswell, John, Christianity, Social Tolerance, and Homosexuality. University of Chicago Press, 1980.

Brannum-Harris, Rod, The Pharisees Amongst Us: How the anti-gay campaign unmasks the religious perpetrators of the campaign to be modern-day Pharisees. BookSurge Publishing, 2006.

Brentlinger, Rick, Gay Christian 101. Brentlinger, 2011 ⟨URL: gaychristian101.com⟩.

Bruce, F.F., The Canon of Scripture. IVP Academic, 1988.

Bruce, Frederick Fyvie, The New Testament Documents: Are They Reliable? Wilder Publications, 2009.

Bullough, Vern L., Sexual Variance in Society and History. University of Chicago Press, 1980.

Cadonau-Huseby, Anita, Leviticus: Pagans, Purity, and Property. WordPress, 2008.

Cameron, James, Titanic. 20th Century Fox;Paramount Pictures;Lightstorm Entertainment, 1997.

Cantarella, Bisexuality in the Ancient World. Yale Press, 1992.

Countryman, L. William, Dirt, Greed, and Sex: Sexual Ethics in the New Testament and

Their Implications for Today. Fortress Press, 2007.

Douglass, Frederick, Narrative of the Life of Frederick Douglass, An American Slave: Written by Himself. Yale University Press, 2001.

Dover, Greek Homosexuality. Harvard University Press, 1989.

Durant, Will, Caesar and Christ - A History of Roman Civilization and of Christianity from their Beginnings to A.D. 323 (Story of Civilization). Simon & Schuster, 1944.

Dynes, Wayne, Racha. The Encyclopedia of Homosexuality edition. Garland, 1990.

Ehrman, Bart D., The New Testament and Other Early Christian Writings. Oxford University Press, 1998.

Fee, Dr. Gordon D., The New International Commentary on the New Testament, The First Epistle To The Corinthians. Eerdmans, 1987.

Ford, Katie and Aarons, Leroy, Prayers for Bobby. Once Upon A Times Films, 2009.

Foundation, Lockman, editor, Greek Dictionary of the New American Standard Exhaustive Concordance. Zondervan, 2000.

Gagnon, Robert, The Bible and Homosexual Practice: Texts and Hermeneutics. Abingdon Press, 2002.

Green, Keith, When I Hear the Praises Start: For Him Who Has Ears to Hear Album. Sparrow Records, 1977.

Greenberg, David F., The Construction of Homosexuality. University of Chicago Press, 1988.

Gutt, Ernst-August, Relevance Theory and Translation: Toward a New Realism in Bible Translation. International Meeting of the Society of Biblical Literature, 2004.

Hanks, Tom, The Subversive Gospel. Pilgrim Press, 2000.

Helminiak, Daniel A., What the Bible Really Says About Homosexuality. Alamo Square Distribution, 2000.

Hemfelt, Robert, Minirth, Frank and Meier, Paul, Love is a Choice: Breaking the Cycle of Addictive Relationships. Monarch Publications, 1990.

Hippolytus; Roberts, Alexander and Donaldson, James, editors, Refutation of All Heresies: Book V.2. Scribners, 1903.

Hoad, T. F., editor, The Concise Oxford Dictionary of English Etymology. Oxford University Press, 1993.

Hoyle, Fred, Mathematics of Evolution. Acorn Enterprises Llc., 1999.

Humana, Charles, The Keeper of the Bed: The Story of the Eunuch. Arlington Books, 1973.

J. McNeill, John, The Church and the Homosexual. Beacon Press, 1993.

Johansson, Warren, Whosoever Shall Say to His Brother, Racha. Volume 10, Cabirion, 1984.

Kuefler, Matthew, The Manly Eunuch. University of Chicago Press, 2001.

Leick, Gwendolyn, Sex and Eroticism in Mesopotamian Literature. Routledge, 2003.

LockmanFoundation, editor, Updated New American Standard Bible. Zondervan Publishing House, 1999.

Mader, Donald, The Entimos Pais of Matthew 8:5-13 and Luke 7:1-10. Harland Publishing, Inc., 1998, Homosexuality and Religion and Philosophy.

Marland Horner, Thomas, Jonathan Loved David: Homosexuality in Biblical Times. Westminster John Knox Press, 1978.

Martin et al., Meanings and Consequences. Biblical Ethics and Homosexuality. Louisville: Westminster Press, 1996.

Martin, Luther, Hellenistic Religions. Oxford University Press, 1987.

Maternus, Firmicus, The Error of Pagan Religions. Newman Press, 1970.

Metzger, Bruce, The Text of the New Testament: Its Transmission, Corruption, and Restoration. 4th edition. Oxford University Press, 2005.

Metzger, Bruce M., The Canon of the New Testament: Its Origin, Development, and Significance. Oxford University Press, April 1997.

Milgrom, Jacob, Leviticus 17-22. The Anchor Yale Bible Commentaries edition. Yale University Press, 2000.

Mills, Watson E.; Idem, editor, Mercer Dictionary of the Bible. Mercer University Press, 1994.

Miner, Jeff and Connoley, John Tyler, The Children are Free. Jesus Metropolitan Community Church, 2002.

Nissinen, Martti, Homoeroticism in the Biblical World. Fortress Press, 1998.

Quakers, Quaker Views - Close Relationships. Quaker Life, 2008.

Quakers, British, Towards a Quaker View of Sex. Quaker Home Service, 1998.

Raymond J., Jr. Lawrence, The Poisoning of Eros: Sexual Values in Conflict. A. Moore Press, 1989.

Rogers, Jack, Jesus, the Bible, and Homosexuality: Explode the Myths, Heal the Church. Westminster John Knox Press, 2006.

Roscoe, Will, Priests of the Goddess: Gender Transgression in Ancient Religion. The University of Chicago, 1996.

Roughgarden, Joan, Evolution's Rainbow: Diversity, Gender, and Sexuality in Nature and People. University of California Press, 2009.

Schneider, Johannes; Kittel, Gerhard, editors, Article on Eunouchos. Theological Dictionary of the New Testament edition. Wm. B. Eerdmans Publishing Company, 1986.

Scofield, Cyrus I., Scofield Reference Bible. Oxford University Press, 1917.

Scroggs, Robin, The New Testament and Homosexuality: Contextual Background for Contemporary Debate. Fortress Press, 1983.

Sergent, Bernard, Homosexuality in Greek Myth. Beacon Press, 1986.

Spetner, Lee M., Not by Chance. Judaica Press, 1997.

Sphero, M.W., Escaping the Shithole: How and Why to Leave a Bad Neighborhood Once and for All. Herms Press, 2009.

Stoner, Peter, Science Speaks: Scientific Proof of the Accuracy of Prophecy and the Bible. Moody Press, 1969.

Stoner, Peter, Science Speaks: Online Edition. November 2005 ⟨URL: `http://www.geocities.com/stonerdon/science_speaks.html`⟩.

Strobel, Lee, The Case for Christ. Zondervan, 1998.

Stryper, Soldiers Under Command album. Hollywood Records, 1985.

Swancutt, Diana, Disease of Effemination: The Charge of Effeminacy and the Verdict of God (Rom. 1:18-2:16). Society of Biblical Literature, 2003.

Thelos, Philo, Divine Sex: Liberating Sex from Religious Tradition. Trafford Publishing, 2006.

Thelos, Philo, God is not a Homophobe: An Unbiased Look at Homosexuality in the Bible. Trafford Publishing, 2006.

Thompson, Frank Charles D.D. Ph.D., editor, Thompson Chain-Reference Bible: New International Version. Zondervan Bible Publishers, 1983.

Townsley, Jeramy, Paul, the Goddess Religions and Queers: Romans 1:23-28. ⟨URL: `http://www.jeramyt.org/papers/paulcybl.html#_edn4`⟩.

Webster, Webster's New Universal Unabridged Dictionary. Barnes & Noble Books, 1992.

Westminster Meeting, Quakers of, statement from. Quakers, 1963.

Wikipedia, List of Christian denominational positions on homosexuality. Wikipedia, 2011 ⟨URL: http://en.wikipedia.org/wiki/ List_of_Christian_denominational_ positions_on_homosexuality⟩.

Williams, Roman Homosexuality : Ideologies of Masculinity in Classical Antiquity. Oxford UP, 1999.

Wilson, Nancy, Our Tribe: Queer Folks, God, Jesus, and the Bible. Alamo Square Distributors, 2000.

Index

247

CPSIA information can be obtained
at www.ICGtesting.com
Printed in the USA
BVHW071646240820
587165BV00005B/111